THE TROUBLE WITH

THE TROUBLE WITH
BARNACLES

BY HORACE L. FENTON JR.

General Director,
Latin America Mission

ZONDERVAN
PUBLISHING HOUSE

OF THE ZONDERVAN CORPORATION
GRAND RAPIDS, MICHIGAN 49506

*To my mother
With thanksgiving to God for all that her godly
example and patient teaching have meant to me*

Contents

AN EX-PRIEST'S DISAPPOINTMENT

THE CITY, AS GOD SEES IT

Introduction

I didn't want to write a book. In a special sense, I didn't want to write *this* book.

Why the antipathy to book-writing? I think I can trace it back to the time, about thirty-five years ago, when I was doing quite a bit of book-reviewing for a well-known Christian journal.

Their book review editor used to send me five or six new books at a time, and I would dutifully plow through them and then write a brief evaluation of each one. I did it because it provided a way to build my library; I wouldn't have been able to buy these books on my limited budget. But it soon became evident that, whether I paid for them or not, most of the books weren't even of a quality to justify taking up space on my bookshelves. Perhaps one book out of five was worth rereading or referring to at some future date.

The rest were junk. They were orthodox; they were evangelical; but they were junk. They said nice things. True things. But they were poorly written, superficial, safe. Many of them seemed to be collections of sermons by pastors whose congregations had said so many nice things about them that the preachers came to believe these well-meaning tributes and committed their homiletical masterpieces to deathless print — where they were shown to be trite, shallow, sterile.

I made up my mind in those days that I would never add to this spate of evangelical trivia. It seemed to me a man ought to have something special to say and a gift for saying it before he put something in book form, expecting God to bless it and the evangelical public to buy it.

I still feel that way. And doubly so about "devotional" books! There seems to be little market for them in our day — a fact which ought to be fairly easy to understand, given the level of much devotional writing. Like much that passes for expository preaching in our time, devotional essays seem to be written in a vacuum — pious comments on "safe" passages of Scripture, with little or no relation to life as people face it and with no attempt to grapple with the real issues that press upon all of us every day.

I am perfectly capable of writing this same kind of trivia, and it seemed to me that the safest thing, therefore, was not to write at all!

Obviously, my thinking along these lines has modified — to the extent that I have come to a sort of grudging willingness to commit myself to print, at least on this one occasion. Perhaps any reader who has followed me this far is entitled to an explanation as to why I momentarily threw off those inhibitions.

Two factors helped change my thinking. One was a friend of many years, Mr. Stephen Slocum, executive assistant to the president of Dallas Theological Seminary and formerly executive secretary of the American Tract Society. Our friendship dates back to the time when he was a student in the Wharton School of Finance of the University of Pennsylvania and I was director of Christian education in his home church.

Through the ensuing years, the Lord has repeatedly drawn us together in various projects, particularly during the time he served as a member of the board of trustees of the Latin America Mission.

In recent years Mr. Slocum has urged me to do some writing for publication. On the basis of the convictions I have mentioned, I held out against him for a long time, only to give in finally to his request to look at some of the devotional articles I had written for some time, chiefly for *The Sunday School Times* and the *Latin America Evangelist*.

Once these articles were in his hands, Mr. Slocum went over them carefully and then insisted that many of them, if reworked and polished, would be well worth putting into book form, together with additional essays of a similar kind. He offered to get in touch with potential publishers. Almost before I knew it, we had reached the contract-signing stage, and here we are!

All of which is not to place on my good friend any responsibility for the contents of this little book, nor is it to blame him for my failure to hold to my convictions. It is to express a real sense of gratitude, however, to a friend who believed that I had something to say to the reading public when I wasn't at all sure that this was the case. Whether or not he was right, I am very grateful for his confidence and for his persistence.

There was one other factor that moved me to change my mind about this business of writing a book. As one grows older (a person does not have to grow old, but he cannot help growing older!) he realizes that every good thing God has given him was meant to be shared. None of his blessings are merely to be selfishly enjoyed; He blesses each of us that others also may be blessed. If that be true (and it can't be otherwise, in the light of Paul's declaration in 2 Corinthians 9:8: "And God is able to give you more than you need, so that you will always have all you need for yourselves and more than enough for every good cause." Today's English Version), then I want to share with others some of the lessons God has been patiently trying to teach me.

Indeed, that has been the nature of my ministry through the years — the simple endeavor to pass on to others what He has so graciously bestowed upon me. As one draws toward the close of his earthly ministry, without knowing whether thirty months or thirty years yet remain, he sees the need of sharing as widely as he can the good things of God.

9

With such a purpose in mind, what better medium than the printed page? And under such circumstances, dare a writer let his long-held inhibitions keep him from passing on that which the Lord, often through others, has passed on to him?

So that's how I came to write the book I didn't want to write. In preparing it, I have been fully conscious of my limitations — limitations which I criticized so strongly in other authors during my book-reviewing days. But a man learns after a while that not only salvation is all of grace but also every subsequent blessing of God has its origin in that same grace. Surely if anything we say or do helps another, we know better than to take the credit for ourselves. Our best efforts to speak, to write, or to act are so tinged with our own human frailty that only a gracious and almighty God can bring good out of them. All of us know that He does just this on occasion, and it is my prayer that He will find a way to glorify Himself and to bless some of His people through the pages of this book.

In addition to my gratitude to Him, I want to express my heartfelt thanks to my colleagues in the work of the Lord, both Latin Americans and North Americans, who have taught me so much of our God and of His ways; to my faithful secretary, Miss Molly Fahringer, who has given countless hours to the preparation of this manuscript; and to my wife, whose encouragement not only in this project but in all of my ministry has been of inestimable help to me.

My own life has been greatly enriched by the reading of many books. Not all of them were worth the time spent on them, but some have helped me to know my Lord better. I shall be grateful to God if something I have written proves of similar help to my brothers and sisters in Christ.

The Trouble With Barnacles

The Trouble With Barnacles

Thanks to modern research, barnacles apparently don't bother ocean-going ships much today. But there was a time when they were the scourge of maritime traffic.

The trouble with barnacles was that most of the time they couldn't be seen. They fastened themselves to the hull of a ship below the waterline, so the vessel became encrusted with these tenacious creatures long before an ordinary observer knew they were there.

Of course, the captain of the ship would know. Over a period of time he was bound to become aware of the accumulated accretions. The ship didn't handle the way it once did, and its speed was substantially reduced. All this was because the vessel carried dead weight that was no part of its real cargo. Something had to be done.

This picture may help us understand the strange action of Christ when, at the beginning of His public ministry, He cleansed the Temple (John 2). (If you don't think His action strange by all human standards, perhaps you have grown insensitive, through long familiarity, to what the Scripture says.)

The pure faith which God meant His people to manifest had become overgrown — encrusted with barnacles. Moreover, the whole thing happened so gradually that even religious men had not noticed. No one seemed to think it strange that the worshipers in the Temple were assailed by the sounds and scents of animals or that it was easier to hear the cries of moneychangers than to hear the voice of God. The situation, which at one time might have shocked sensitive men, passed unnoticed by everyone.

Everyone, that is, except Jesus. The Captain of the ship knew the difference the barnacles made. Christ recognized that drastic action was called for.

From our vantage point in history, we easily see how the religion of the Jews in Christ's day had become encrusted with foreign objects and how God's truth was all but hidden by these accretions. Yet it seldom occurs to us that over the years we have allowed our own faith to become covered with barnacles we do not recognize. We have nothing so obvious as bleating sheep and cooing pigeons to call our attention to what we have superimposed on the message of the New Testament.

We mean to proclaim, "Believe on the Lord Jesus Christ, and thou shalt be saved." But what we often say is, "Believe on the Lord Jesus Christ and accept our cultural patterns, our economic, political, and social outlook, our views of baptism and of the Holy Spirit, our interpretation of prophecy, our organizational relationships — and thou shalt be saved."

We do not realize we have lost the simplicity of the Gospel. What we think is a direct, forthright message more often sounds to the unbelieving world like a complicated, confusing business — a message cluttered with qualifications and corrupted by footnotes and appendices. We too often give to cultural or social convictions—inherited or otherwise acquired—the same standing as the scriptural truths we have received from God by revelation. Sometimes people are kept from the Savior, not by the offense of the cross, but by the offense of the things we have added to the cross. God's true message is hidden by the accretions we have allowed to accumulate.

That's the trouble with barnacles. They build up unnoticed. Then comes a day when they must be dealt with — ruthlessly. If the religious people of Christ's day had only seen what happened to their faith and had done something about it, His act of judgment would have been unnecessary. The Temple once again would have become a place where men met God, unhindered in their worship by the distractions of other sights and sounds.

We need a fresh, hard look at our own faith — an objective discernment of the difference between what God has revealed and what we have added to it. If the sin of liberalism has been the attempt to subtract from the revelation of God, it may well be that the sin of evangelicals is too often an unwitting attempt to add to it. That we have done this without realizing it is no excuse.

The trouble with barnacles is that they do their deadly work, whether or not they are seen.

False Economy

Economy is a virtue — usually. But there is a kind of false economy; it wastes, rather than saves, precious resources.

When an army tries to economize on its ammunition, it may well be on the road to inglorious defeat. A farmer who sows sparingly reaps sparingly. He has economized at the wrong place, and he loses rather than gains, by his mistaken attempt to save.

When will we Christians learn that lesson? Paul taught it long ago. Our experience confirms what the Spirit said through him. Yet we go on trying to do the Lord's work on a shoestring — with a minimum of all-out effort.

If we persist on this disastrous course, at least let us have the honesty not to call it economy. Let us preserve our integrity by recognizing it for what it really is: waste. Let us stop pretending that we are serious about fulfilling the Great Commission in our generation. And let us not be surprised at the pathetic paucity of our reaping.

We dare not continue to carry out the work of the Lord at our present slow, ineffectual pace. Thank God that in recent years the Lord's people in Latin America have awakened, through Evangelism-in-Depth, to the scriptural truth that abundant reaping must be preceded by abundant sowing. That is a relatively simple statement, but it has profound implications. Let's look at some of them.

As Kenneth Strachan pointed out years ago, more national pastors and missionaries are needed everywhere, but the mere multiplication of their numbers is not the answer to world evangelization. To train more national pastors, to send out missionaries, is good, but it does not constitute really abundant sowing. And it will not produce the abundant harvest that God purposes and longs for.

Nothing less than the total mobilization of all believers will do. Nothing else is worthy of being called "abundant sowing." Anything else is false economy.

This means that each one of us who knows Christ is meant to be more deeply involved in the work of the Gospel than we are now. It means we need to be mobilized and trained to share our faith with relatives, friends, and other acquaintances who do not know Christ.

But it means much more than this. It means God calls every child of His to give top priority to world evangelization — to make it his supreme passion that men everywhere shall have an adequate opportunity to know what God offers them, through the death and resurrection of His Son.

We have not even begun to approach the task this way. We have left the job to the professionals or to the "dedicated Christians," an elite minority of concerned believers. We have sown sparingly — and our harvests have inevitably been proportionate to our sowing. This is false economy, and it is not worthy of our professed allegiance to Jesus Christ.

We fall under the same condemnation in regard to finances. The evangelization of the world is a costly business; there is no point even to talk about it unless we are willing to pay the price.

In Latin America the Evangelism-in-Depth programs of recent years have been wonderfully effective in expediting the spread of the Gospel in several countries. It is utterly amazing what is accomplished on budgets that are, relatively speaking, a pittance compared to the job to be done. Thanks be to God for the way He has multiplied what has been put in His hands.

But the principle of sowing and reaping still applies. The Lord's work in every part of the world will be more fruitful when God's people recognize the need for sowing abundantly and when this recognition is reflected in their bank balances.

We pride ourselves, in our day, on the number of wonderful new media available for the spread of the Gospel. We rejoice in these tools — yet do not begin to use them to their full potential. We gear the spread of the Gospel, by and large, to the horse-and-buggy pace of an earlier age.

It is not that victory in God's work is to be won by gimmicks and gadgets. But to have God-given tools available and not use them for His glory can scarcely be anything but sin.

Think, for example, of television. This is a tool which the experts say has incalculable potential for disseminating knowledge, for influencing human behavior, for summoning men to decisions. It is a neutral tool, capable of almost infinite evil or immeasurable good, depending on how it is used and who uses it.

Yet how many examples can you cite of its being used, creatively and effectively, to confront men with their awful need and with God's bounteous provision? Our sporadic, often ill-planned invasions of this field can only be called meager sowing. We reveal thereby a lack of seriousness about making Christ known to the multitudes.

It would be easy to multiply illustrations of our false economy, but it shouldn't be necessary. Someday — and it had better be soon! — we Christians will become ashamed of having economized at the one place where it was eternal folly to do so: in the work of making Christ known. When that day comes, we will know in practice what now is only pious theory to most of us — that abundant reaping requires abundant sowing. Anything less is false economy.

On Being Helpful to Others and Useful for Christ

Every homemaker knows the predicament of having company arrive just when the family larder looks like Old Mother Hubbard's cupboard. Our Lord Jesus was surely touching a responsive chord in the hearts of His hearers when He told them the story of the host who in desperation awoke a friend at midnight, seeking something with which to feed his unforeseen guest.

When we think of that passage (Luke 11:5-13), we usually see its chief message as persistence in prayer. Indeed, our Lord was emphasizing that in this parable.

But there is a secondary lesson here, too. Jesus' words show us how we may meet the needs of others and thus be useful to Him. I need to learn that lesson, and maybe you do, too! Once our primary question was "How may I know eternal life?" Now that we know the Lord, we ought to ask, "How may I be helpful to men and useful for Christ?" Our Scripture passage gives this answer.

Note, first of all, our predicament. It is formed of two elements: we are surrounded by tremendous need, and we are conscious of our utter inability to meet it.

You know that all around you are people in great need, looking to you for help, don't you? If you don't perhaps you are asleep! Like Jonah, you rest peacefully in the bottom of the boat while all your companions struggle amid a terrible storm which threatens their very existence. Or it may be you have so cut yourself off from unsaved men and have so little "sinner contact" that your needy neighbors dare not approach you in their time of trouble. Like many other Christians, you are not of the world, but you are not in the world, either! Perhaps you're living in an insulated ghetto, unable to feel the suffering of people around you.

Thank God, it isn't that way with all Christians. Recently I met some folks who had made it their business to keep a loving contact with a Roman Catholic family in their neighborhood. They haven't pressured the Catholics, or badgered them, or argued with them; they have been good neighbors for Christ's sake. A few weeks ago, when tragedy struck that Catholic family, they turned to their evangelical neighbors, welcoming in the hour of their need a sure word about God's eternal life. You see, there is need on every hand if we are only alert to it.

But even when we see the need, we are conscious of our inability to meet it. We are empty — and we might as well admit it. We know the Gospel, but a mere recitation of its facts, apart from divine power, is a poor substitute for bread. Yes, we have a testimony, but the glib recital of it may mock, rather than feed, our needy friends. The trouble is, people are always seeking our help at midnight, when our larder is bare — and the stores are all closed!

Next, look at our *alternatives*. We may turn away the hungry, unfed. Many Christians do today. Involved in a never-ending round of "spiritual" activities, they feel no sense of responsibility for needy people whose lives they touch every day. Like the Priest and the Levite on the Jericho road, they pass by the needy in their hurry to do "religious duties."

Or we may seek help in the right place. Christ's counsel to us in Luke's passage is clear: "Go to ONE who can meet your need and your friend's and ask him." Go, ask! To do that, you must know what you need and where to get it. Seek! Don't bemoan your poverty — seek His riches. Knock! Unashamedly call attention to your desperate plight. Christ guarantees that this is the way to get what you'll need.

Having seen our predicament and our alternatives, let's look at our confidence. Its basis is that God is committed to provide what we need. Even the sleepy householder did that, though irked at the battering on his door at midnight. God says we "shall not want any good thing" (Ps. 34:10). He'll supply all our needs (Phil. 4:19). He will provide what we need so that we can provide for the needy who look to us for help. Do you know what that means? Our excuses for not being useful to Him are based, not in humility, but in unbelief.

God will do more. He will provide what we need most — Himself! The promise of the Holy Spirit in Luke 11:13 is one of the greatest in the Bible. Our basic need is not strength, courage, patience, or a host of other things, but the Holy Spirit, producing these and all other virtues in us. Don't lose this glorious promise in a dispute about terminology. It's possible to have an icily correct doctrine of the Holy Spirit and no daily experience of His power. What you need, to make you useful, is the Spirit's fullness.

God will give Him, in fresh measure, to those who ask for Him. This is the prayer God never says no to. In the light of His promise, no excuse for unfruitfulness is valid. You can be helpful to others and useful to Him. Then ask, right now, and ask each day for His best gift — the Holy Spirit.

21

How to Rebuke the Devil

She was a frail little lady, and she approached me after a service at a summer Bible conference.

"You were speaking today about the seminary in Costa Rica," she began. "How much does it cost to support one of those students?"

When I cited the then current figure of $25 a month, she was obviously disappointed. "Oh," she said, "I had hoped it would be less and that I could support one." She explained that she was in straitened circumstances: a widow living on a small pension and her Social Security, plus the rent from two rooms in her home in Camden, New Jersey. Besides, she pointed out, her tithe — and more — was long since committed to other worthy causes.

So there was nothing she could do about a student in Costa Rica — until a different thought struck her. "Do you ever accept half the support of a student?" she asked. When I replied yes, she said, "Then I'll trust the Lord to send me an additional $12.50 a month, so I can have a part in one of those students."

I thanked her and assured her that when she sent in her first month's gift I'd give her the name of "her" student and tell her a bit about his background, so she could pray intelligently for him. She was excited about the prospect.

Next morning I gave another missionary message at the conference, and immediately after the service I was met again by the same little old lady. She reminded me that she had been talking to me about taking on half the support of a student — as though I might have forgotten her already! Then she said, "Ever since we discussed this matter yesterday morning, the devil has been talking to me about the commitment I made to you — and for the first time in his life, he's telling the truth!"

I was puzzled — as she obviously intended I should be — and asked her what the devil had told her. "He tells me," she replied, "that I can't afford to carry out my commitment, and he's telling the truth — I just can't do it."

She recited the same story she had told me the previous day, a tale of very limited resources, long since over-committed. The devil was, indeed, telling the truth for once!

Anxious to relieve her mind, I said, "Believe me, I understand your situation fully, and the Lord understands it perfectly. After all, you didn't sign any contract, and you don't need to apologize to me or anybody else for your inability to do what, on the spur of the moment, you thought you could carry through. God knows your limitations, and you don't need to reproach yourself just because you can't do all that you would like to do. So please don't think about it anymore; the Lord will provide for our students in some other way."

I thought I was setting her mind at ease, but it didn't work that way. A look of consternation crossed her face — she disagreed violently with what I had said. "Oh, no!" she remonstrated. "That isn't why I told you about my conversation with the devil. What I really wanted to tell you was this: I have decided that the only way I can rebuke that old Enemy is by telling you this morning that I'm going to trust God to enable me to take on the *full* support of a student. After all, I might as well trust Him for $25.00 a month as for $12.50! I'll show Satan that he can't tell me what I can or can't do for the Lord."

And she did. Month by month thereafter, her letter

would arrive, always accompanied by a check and always brimming over with thanksgiving to God for His faithfulness. "Praise the Lord with me," she would write. "He did it again, and here's the $25 for this month's support. Tell Agustin I'm praying for him."

I remember one month when she wrote, "Isn't the Lord wonderful? He knew that Agustin's birthday is this month, so He sent me $30 this time — $25 for his support and $5 for a birthday present." For three years she bore monthly testimony to God's faithfulness and to her love for Him and for Agustin.

She did indeed rebuke the devil. She did it by refusing to believe the enemy's assessment of what she could do. He is past master at reminding us of our limitations and weaknesses. He often tells us the truth about them — in ourselves we are at least as useless and weak as he says. But now and then God has someone like the little old lady from Camden, who acknowledges the truth concerning herself but refuses to believe God can't do something about it.

See, the way to rebuke the devil is to get our eyes off him and off ourselves, too, so we may fix them on a Savior who is not limited by our limitations nor discouraged by our failures. He is still "able to do exceeding abundantly above all that we ask or think" (Eph. 3:20). He still has the power to "make you perfect in every good work to do His will" (Heb. 13:21).

The devil is never to be trusted — even when he is telling the truth. He never has our welfare at heart, and he has no concern for the world for which Christ died. So he tries to make us believe we cannot go beyond what we have already done for Christ; he does this by causing us to forget the power available to us in our Savior — a power which more than compensates for our inadequacies.

God's greatest servants are not powerful people but weaklings, like my little friend, who dare to believe

Christ is not limited by their shortcomings. Believing, they become living proof that it is true, and so may you. You may trust Him to do the impossible in you and to do the impossible through you. Your life will then, likewise, be a rebuke to the devil.

A Sequel to "How to Rebuke the Devil"

In the preceding pages, we met a little old lady who dared to rebuke the devil. That wasn't the whole story, so here is a sequel. Yet even after the sequel is told, the story will be unfinished, for when one does something for Christ with His blessing, the story goes on and on — and on. In a sense it never ends. Thus, the sequel — but not the end of the story.

When the first gift, postmarked CAMDEN, NEW JERSEY, arrived from my friend, I wrote to her about Agustin, "her" student. He was in his first year in the seminary and had come from the Canary Islands — thousands of miles from San Jose, Costa Rica. For three long years he would be separated from his family and friends, so I encouraged his newfound supporter in the States to pray for him faithfully as he faced homesickness and discouragement in the months ahead.

She was more than faithful, both with her gifts and with her prayers. Three years later Agustin graduated and returned to his homeland to serve Christ in Spain. There he became the head of a small Bible institute and found his joy in training other young people for Christ's service. He was multiplying himself spiritually, and the investment of the little lady from Camden was paying rich dividends. The Lord had multiplied her gifts and answered her prayers in ways she hadn't anticipated. An almighty God was at work, constantly increasing the value of her investment.

But this isn't the end of the story. It isn't even the end of the sequel! Soon after Agustin returned home, he urged a young friend to go to Costa Rica to prepare himself for Christian service. The two friends discussed the matter at length and prayed earnestly for the Lord's leading. In due time Plutarco made the journey across the water and enrolled in the seminary where his friend had done so well.

It soon became apparent to the faculty that Plutarco was a brilliant student, a young man with great potential. Within a few years he graduated from both the seminary and the University of Costa Rica. More amazing was the fact that both institutions promptly invited him to join their faculties. In the seminary he taught New Testament; in the University, philosophy. He bore a faithful witness to Christ at both schools, and his work was blessed by the Lord and deeply appreciated by his colleagues and students.

He used his furlough times for graduate studies and became increasingly effective in his teaching ministry. Like his friend, Agustin, he was multiplying himself in the lives of others and becoming an additional dividend on the investment that an elderly lady had made at a Bible conference.

There came the day when Plutarco was chosen by the Latin America Mission and the seminary faculty to be the rector (president) of that school. He accepted the appointment, with the understanding that he would be permitted to continue teaching part-time in the university — a stipulation arising from his love for philosophy and his deep desire to represent Jesus Christ on a secular campus, where a witness to Him was all too rare.

Permission was gladly granted. He ministered on both campuses until late 1971, when he left for Greece and doctoral studies at the University of Athens. His academic goal was high, but his vision remained unchanged: he resolved to go back to Costa Rica to serve Jesus Christ in teaching young people. Some of those young people have already come to know the

Savior and look forward to serving Him; others have never met Him but may someday get a glimpse of the Lord through a servant of His, their philosophy professor.

So that's the end of the sequel to the story of the little old lady who rebuked the devil. But obviously the story itself hasn't ended. As long as Agustin and Plutarco allow the Lord to use them to introduce others to Christ and to train them for the Lord's service, the story will go on — long after the original participants have passed from the earthly scene. The little old lady is already at home with the Lord, and someday the earthly labors of Agustin and Plutarco will be over, too. But the original investment will still be paying dividends. The story will not end.

Perhaps that's what the poet meant when he wrote, ". . . Only what's done for Christ will last."

The Christian View of Detachment

"Detachment" isn't a biblical word. You won't find it in your concordance. But though the word doesn't appear in our English versions, the concept is there. For example, Paul devotes a whole section of his letter to the Philippians to this idea. He's writing about detachment. Not just from sin; nor merely from questionable things; but from that obsession with ourselves and our possessions which often limits and even destroys our concern for others!

The apostle first exhorts us to a life of detachment by citing the example of our Lord Jesus, who willingly emptied Himself for our sakes (Phil. 2:4, 5, 7). Then Paul rejoices that Timothy is characterized by this same quality (vv. 19, 20). He laments that, among all the other Christians he knows, this sort of detachment seems to be a forgotten virtue (v. 21).

It's still scarce! In most of us our conversion, however genuine, has not been allowed to go very deep. We have become detached from our sins — at least from the most noticeable of them. We have probably made a clean break with some of the "questionable" things. But to let go of the *legitimate*, for Christ's sake, is as rare a thing now as it was in Paul's time.

Yet this virtue is intended to be a distinctive characteristic of anyone who names Christ. To his brethren at Philippi, Paul writes, "Let this mind be in you, which was also in Christ Jesus." He goes to some length to demonstrate the detachment of our Lord. From Christ we learn that:

1. The best preaching is by example. The unselfishness of the Lord Jesus, His readiness to

exchange His heavenly glory for the suffering and loneliness of the Incarnation — this is better than a thousand sermons on detachment. Timothy's concern for others, all too rare, is a more effective exhortation than a host of articles on the subject. The world today doesn't need our bewailing of its selfishness. It does need to see unselfish, detached lives. It needs men not charmed by the appeal of material things. New Testament truths are always in need of translation, not into some new idiom, but into life.

2. Detachment, in a Christian sense, is often from legitimate things. Our Lord Jesus was holy and undefiled, fully separated from sin. He was detached from more than sin: from a great host of things which were rightly His from all eternity, things He was not duty-bound to disconnect Himself from. These were things He might have grasped, but He chose otherwise. For us, doing God's will may likewise mean forswearing ambitions, ideals, and aspirations, letting go much that is legitimate, remembering "no man that warreth entangleth himself with the affairs of this life" (2 Tim. 2:4) — not even the good things! Warfare demands this kind of disconnection.

3. Detachment is progressive. Somewhere in the counsels of eternity our Lord Jesus willed to do the Father's will by giving Himself for our salvation. But that decision, made once for all, had to be reaffirmed in new and more difficult circumstances throughout His earthly life. And so it is with us. We may have determined long since to surrender ourselves completely to the Lordship of Christ, to be free from anything that would qualify or limit that commitment. But such

matters may not be settled once and for all. Our original decision needs constant reaffirmation. We need to keep saying yes to Christ, and no to anything that threatens to divert us from whole-hearted devotion to Him. Our growth and effectiveness for Christ will be determined by the measure of our ever-increasing detachment from all that hinders us in fulfilling His will.

4. Detachment brings reward. The reward may not be immediate, but it is sure. "God also hath highly exalted him" (Phil. 2:9). The Father always pours Himself out on His detached ones. They are God's rich people who, having nothing, possess all things. But they possess them by a constant vigilance against slavery to those appeals which offer a pleasure which, like sin itself, is but for a season.

Is detachment a forgotten virtue in your life?

Survival Isn't Enough!

It's an old story, but it still carries a message for Christians. A girl was jubilantly telling how, so soon after graduating from a training course in first aid, she had opportunity to put her skills into practice.

"It was an amazing thing," she said. "One night, less than a week after finishing the course, I was walking home when I came upon the scene of a terrible accident. An old man had lost control of his car and it had smashed into a tree beside the road. He was obviously badly hurt, and no one seemed to be doing anything about it. He had been thrown out of his car and was bleeding profusely.

"It suddenly occurred to me how fortunate it was that I had just completed my first-aid course. I recalled the particular lesson which taught us that, if we were in danger of fainting, the head should be lowered to a position between the knees, and the danger would be averted. So I did what I had been taught to do, and it worked — I didn't faint! How glad I was for my lessons in first aid!"

The story may be hard to believe, but its spiritual parallel is all too familiar. So many of us seem to think survival is itself a virtue — no matter what happens to anyone else. And so we speak enthusiastically of our conversion, as though our salvation were an end in itself and as though we dared to rejoice in it without giving a thought to others who still don't know Christ. When we become so self-centered, we are settling for our own spiritual survival, as though this were all God had in mind when He saved us. But in His glorious purpose, survival isn't enough!

Our attitude as individual Christians is reflected in our churches. Too often we look on the local fellowship of Christians as a sort of spiritual bomb shelter, where we can hide away from an explosion-rocked world. There we gather as often as we can, join hands with fellow believers, and sing "Safe Am I" — hoping for the time when the bombs won't fall anymore and meanwhile counting on the church walls to protect us from worldly evils.

If only we could see ourselves as God sees us, we'd recognize how often we are passionately devoted to self-survival — as if this were a goal bound to please the Lord. Frequently our only concern seems to be to enjoy our salvation, to protect ourselves from contamination, and to wait for the coming of the Lord. Meanwhile, the world for which Christ died still perishes without Him.

Actually we are as blind as the girl who thought her first-aid course was only for her own benefit. Blind, that is, to everything except that which seems to guarantee our own security.

Many of us who claim to rejoice in the promise of Christ's coming are really concerned only with hanging on until that great event takes place. Now, endurance is a biblical virtue and therefore not to be despised; but God has a higher purpose than mere perseverance for His waiting people.

It may well be that the old gospel song, "Hold the fort, for I am coming, " helped perpetuate the unbiblical concept that self-survival is itself a worthy aim for a Christian. It pictures Christ's church as a beleaguered army, trying not to give up any territory it has gained and desperately struggling to hold on until its Captain returns with deliverance.

The New Testament picture is very different. In it we are called, not to hold the fort, but to storm the gates of hell, in the name of Christ and by His power.

33

Our Lord sees His waiting church, not as a group of terrified believers hoping against hope that they can hang on until He comes back, but as a conquering army claiming once again for Him territory which the Evil One has too long usurped.

We are called, as Christ's disciples, not to survival but to service; not to hanging on but to dogged advance; not to a selfish rejoicing in our own salvation but to a Godlike concern for those who do not yet experience the life which has come to mean so much to us.

It's easy to condemn the shortsightedness of the girl who thought that by avoiding fainting she had justified her long hours of studying first aid. It's harder to see that as Christians we are often just like her; yet in our case the consequences may be even more tragic.

The Indians in Your Neighborhood

On Recognizing Them

He is an outstanding leader in the evangelical world, a man for whom I have great respect. So I was delighted to encounter him, his wife, and a friend of hers unexpectedly after being out of touch with him for some years. It was a welcome opportunity for renewed fellowship, and we made the most of it.

As we rejoiced together in the Lord's faithfulness, I asked him to tell me some of his recent experiences in the service of Christ. I wasn't exactly prepared for the way he began —

"You know," he said, "the Lord has been giving my wife and me the most wonderful time reaching the Auca Indians in our neighborhood!" Now, I know well the lovely suburb where they live, and I just could not reconcile my concept of that area with the idea of Auca Indians.

"Look," I said, "the Aucas of South America I know something about, but who are the Aucas in your neighborhood?"

Obviously pleased that his statement had shaken me a bit, he replied, "Why our town is just *filled* with Auca Indians! They are people utterly untouched by the Gospel. They have as little knowledge of its message as any Stone Age tribe in Latin America. They don't go near any churches, and usually the Christians don't go near them. In fact, the most evangelical believers I know seem to have written them off, figuring they are of a completely different culture and utterly uninterested in the Gospel."

"Believe me," he said, speaking with a measure of

deep feeling, "they are really untouched. They might just as well be living in some remote jungle of Ecuador!"

I now saw what he meant, and I listened with eager interest as he told me about these North American "Aucas."

About two years before, he said, the Lord had awakened his wife and him to the fact that they were living in the midst of "Aucas"; He had laid a special burden on their hearts for getting to these people whom no one else was reaching. Together the couple prayed earnestly about their burden, asking the Lord to show them His way of making contact with these needy people.

They decided to begin inviting some of the neighbors to dinner in their home. My friend assured me they didn't put any special Bible texts on the dining room wall for these particular occasions, nor did they insist that their guests listen to a sermon before being fed.

Instead, the couple purposed to show that they cared about the "Aucas" as persons. They asked God for readiness to speak when the Lord wanted them to, and for restraint from speaking when the time for such talk was not right. Above all, they prayed that the love of Christ might be poured out upon their guests.

The results were interesting — to put it mildly! There was a succession of dinner guests, and in a sense each experience was unique. Sometimes the conversation would take an unanticipated turn, and a wonderful opportunity (which seemed very natural, because it was so supernatural) opened up. This led to a fruitful discussion of Christ and of the eternal difference He makes in the lives of those who trust Him.

On other occasions, an evening of pleasant fellowship would pass with no reference to the Savior. This was not because my friends missed their opportunity or were afraid to speak out for Christ, but because the Holy Spirit Himself restrained them. In such cases, they would be sure to invite their guests back. Sometimes on the second occasion, sometimes on the third, there was suddenly an opening; and a couple of Aucas would hear the Good News for the first time.

Then the Aucas began to invite the couple to their homes — and that was something different! As my friend put it, "They surely live in a different world — different standards, different customs, different ambitions. Everything was different."

But he and his wife had determined not to allow anything to upset or intimidate them. This is how he expressed it: "We asked God not to allow these secondary matters to affect us, and we decided that they could blow their smoke in our faces, or they could pour their cocktails over our heads, if they wanted to — provided God would only give us the chance to show them that we loved them for Jesus' sake."

One by one, the Aucas began to respond to the Gospel. Lowering his voice to a whisper, my friend called my attention to the woman conversing with his wife nearby. Joyfully he reported, "Just a few months ago, she was an Auca Indian, and now she is a child of God with a wonderful faith in her newfound Savior."

He added that the woman's husband was not yet a believer, but they were meeting him in New York that night; after dinner together they were going to hear Billy Graham. "Just think," he said, "tonight may be the night when another Auca comes into the kingdom!"

As it turned out, the man made no decision that night, but some months later he made a clear-cut surrender to Christ. After a couple of years, my friend glowingly reported to me, "Those two have become the best missionaries we could ever hope for — among the people of their own tribe!"

I've seldom seen a Christian happier than my friend was that night, telling me of the wonderful things the Lord continued to do among the Aucas of the suburbs. His story did not focus on a special technique, and he was careful to give all the glory to the Lord for what had happened.

Yet as I listened I had a feeling God worked in this way because He found a couple of His children who were sensitive enough to His viewpoint to know that not all the Aucas live in exotic, faraway places, shut off from the Gospel by dense jungles and tropical rivers. There are Aucas everywhere, if only we would see them. These are well-dressed Indians, affluent savages, cultured agnostics, living within sight and sound of the Gospel but neither seeing or hearing it. It is as though they lived in the heart of a South American forest, untouched by the rest of the world.

Surely Aucas in the United States have a real measure of personal responsibility for their failure to respond to the truth so readily available to them. But what of the greater responsibility of people like you and me, who, knowing Christ, have not recognized the Indians in our own neighborhoods — or, having recognized them, have abandoned them to their godless fate?

The story my friend told me that night thrilled me, but his experience ought not to be such a rare thing. More of us ought to be recognizing the Indians in our own neighborhoods and allowing ourselves to be the channels by which God's love is poured out upon them.

On Reaching Them

Reading the preceding chapter may give you some idea who the Indians in your neighborhood are. But recognizing them, important as that is, is not the same as reaching them. And reaching them is our business if we belong to Christ.

Reaching Indians is never easy. While our work in Latin America has been primarily among Spanish-speaking people, I have seen enough of Indian work to know that it's almost invariably hard going. So I am not disposed to tell you that reaching the Indians in your neighborhood will be easy; nor is there a neat little formula to guarantee you success.

In fact, it occurs to me that you will face the very same obstacles we confront in reaching Indians if you let God give you a concern for reaching the tribe in your hometown. I want to touch upon one of these difficulties now.

The first big obstacle missionaries face in evangelizing the Indians of Latin America is geography. Few Indians live in large cities, and they don't come to our churches or our mass meetings. Instead they group together in little villages, scattered on the mountainsides or hidden away in jungles, far from the centers of civilization.

I remember driving along in a jeep in Guatemala one day when my host pointed out to me the little clumps of Indian houses, clinging perilously to the sides of the volcanic mountains. There were roads to a few of these villages, only rough paths to most, and no visible means of access to the rest. I was suddenly conscious of what a barrier geography is to the fulfillment of the Great Commission.

Sometime later I learned that two of my colleagues

had gone to one of these villages. It was only fourteen miles away, and there were roads of a sort. But in a sturdy jeep it still took them seven hours to get there! When they arrived, they found a mere handful of Indians. Yet these were people for whom Christ died, and there is a fair chance the Indians would have never heard the Gospel if my friends had not gone.

This is my point: the obstacle of geography is overcome only when Christians are willing to go where the Indians are. Not many of us will do that — it takes too much time and energy. Anyhow, we'd prefer to be in the "safe" company of fellow Christians, enjoying sweet fellowship rather than trying to overcome the geographical barriers.

You see, even in our country we have that kind of obstacle. There is no lack of roads; the "Indians" here are all within relatively easy reach. Yet the ones who live just a half a block from us might as well be isolated in a jungle village, miles away, for all the meaningful contact we have with them. They are not here in our churches; they are not here, in any great numbers, in our evangelistic crusades. They are Out There, separated from us by geography.

Indians will never be reached for Christ by insisting that they come to where we are. The only way to overcome the obstacle of geography is by going where the Indians are.

Most Christians in the United States do not seem to realize this truth — so the Indians in our neighborhoods remain unreached. But now and then I meet some of God's choice servants who care enough about the Indians to go where they are.

There was the young Christian on a secular college campus in western Pennsylvania, for example. He had invited me to speak to his Inter-Varsity chapter. I arrived on campus about 5:00 P.M. and went to his dormitory room. When he responded to my knock, it was evident that I had awakened him from sleep; he apologized for not being ready, explaining he stayed up all night studying for an exam, then after taking it tumbled into bed and overslept.

As I waited for him to dress, I was startled by a roar just outside the room. A loud voice, apparently calling to someone down the hall, shouted, "Hey, Joe, has Elmer Gantry arrived yet?" I had a strange feeling the voice was talking about me! Just then the man who asked the question burst into my friend's room, and I immediately realized he was the roommate.

He suddenly quieted down when he saw me, and my friend introduced us. I suppose my new acquaintance was satisfied that Elmer Gantry had indeed arrived! That night, as I was having dinner with my Christian friend prior to the Inter-Varsity meeting, I said, "I gather that your roommate is not a Christian." He quickly replied, "You can say that again!"

I asked him how they became roommates, and he replied, almost as though he himself was surprised at what he was saying, "I *asked* for him." He explained how, at the end of his junior year, he had asked the Lord if he couldn't, please, for just one year, have a Christian as a roommate. After three years of it, he was tired of living in a godless atmosphere, of being at the mercy of non-Christian, unsympathetic, and often antagonistic roommates.

It seemed a reasonable enough thing to ask of the Lord, that for just one year he might have a roommate with whom he could pray, study the Word, and have all the joys of Christian fellowship.

Strangely, the Lord said, "No." Although my friend persisted in prayer, he received nothing but a negative response. He finally realized that the Lord was saying, "This campus is full of people who will never go to church to hear My Gospel. They are not likely to attend Christian group meetings, large or small. They

43

may not even listen to a testimony concerning Me. They need someone willing to live with them, for my sake — a Christian willing to forgo the delights of Christian fellowship and to expose himself, day and night, to people who will misunderstand him, criticize him and ridicule him.

"He has to be willing to take all this — just because these unbelievers may never have another contact with the Gospel except what they see and hear in him. Now, will you do it?"

My friend accepted the Lord's challenge and he asked the college authorities to assign a non-Christian as his roommate. He confessed that on many occasions thereafter he momentarily regretted his decision, when he found the "heathen" atmosphere of his room almost unbearable and longed desperately to escape to a place of Christian fellowship.

But there was no escape, not if an Indian was both to see and hear the Gospel. My student friend had learned what the church has almost forgotten: if Indians are to be reached you have to go where they are. It's a costly business, but there is no cut-rate way to overcome the obstacle of geography.

While Christ's gracious invitation to the sinner is to come, His urgent command to the believer is to go. None of us is really what Christ wants us to be until we have heard — and obeyed — both commands.

The Indians in your neighborhood will not come to you. You will have to go to them. You won't always enjoy doing that. Other nicer things will take over your available time if you allow them to do so. And you will be tempted to begrudge the time that it takes to go to the Indians and to be with them, when you would much prefer to be with your Christian friends.

But be assured — those Indians are never going to be reached unless somebody goes to them. It may well be that God is asking, "Will you go?"

On Learning Their Language

If the geographical barrier were the only one we had to overcome to reach the Indians in our neighborhoods, we would breathe a sigh of relief once we had conquered that obstacle.

But in Latin America we have learned there are other equally formidable difficulties that complicate the reaching of the Indians; we will soon discover that the same thing is true in North America. Besides geography, there is the linguistic barrier.

The Indians do not speak our language — and they are not likely to hear us until we learn to speak theirs!

In Guatemala some years ago, as part of a nationwide evangelistic effort, a two-week series of meetings was planned for one small tribe of Indians. No evangelist who could speak their language was available, so it was decided to have the preaching in Spanish, with a bilingual Indian interpreting the message into the language of his tribe.

It was a good idea, but it did not work. Through the first week the Indians sat unmoved as they heard the messages, first in Spanish and then in their own tongue. At week's end the local committee decided things just could not go on this way; some better alternative had to be found.

Their solution: they took a promising Indian who had never preached before, taught him a simple gospel message each afternoon, then prayed for him as he delivered it each night. He was not impressive as a preacher, and he often stumbled as he gave his memorized message. But the people heard the Gospel in their own language, and they responded to it. A number of them came to know Christ.

You see, Indians have to hear the Gospel in their own language — and that goes for the Indians in your neighborhood, too. Most of the time our witnessing to them has been in our language, and it has fallen on their ears like a foreign tongue. No wonder the Indians haven't responded!

Part of the problem is that we think everyone understands our pious language — but they don't. So we prattle on in rolling phrases which often cover our own ignorance of biblical truth and which certainly do not communicate the Good News to Indians. Dr. Samuel Moffett says that frequently when we mention redemption, the worldling thinks only in terms of green stamps!

But the linguistic obstacle is more than just a matter of our using our own religious jargon and thinking everyone should be able to understand it. The problem is deeper; we frequently are not speaking on the Indians' wave length because we haven't bothered to learn what concerns them, what weighs them down, what they feel is making life an intolerable burden for them.

You learn a new language by listening to it. That is the procedure for learning an Indian dialect, and it is also the only way one ever learns to speak the language of another man's heart.

When will we Christians learn that the best prelude to speaking is listening, especially when we are trying to communicate with an Indian? Could it be that the Apostle James had the reaching of Indians in mind when he said, "Let every man be swift to hear, slow to speak" (James 1:19)? We learn by listening.

But we are too busy to listen. As a result, we witness but we do not communicate; we talk *at* the Indians, not *to* them.

In a camp for Christian college students, I spoke one

night on the importance of listening to those whom we want to reach for Christ. I pointed out that our Lord Jesus asked His disciples who men said He was. He knew what men were saying, but He wanted His followers to listen carefully to the opinions men had about Him, even when their ideas were a million miles off target.

The next morning in the staff prayer meeting, one of the camp leaders said to me, "That was a good message you gave last night, but you'd better give it tonight again!" He explained that immediately after the message the night before, he went to the prayer group which was in his charge. Before the meeting got under way, one anguished student said, "Fellows, I need help."

He started to pour out his heart. But before he had said a half-dozen words, several other students interrupted to give him their glib answers to his problem. Inevitably they failed to speak to his need because they had not listened to his heart.

What would you think of a doctor who treated you that way? Suppose you went to his office, greatly concerned about your personal condition, and discovered that he did not care to listen to your symptoms nor to submit you to any tests. Instead, supremely confident that he already knew what was the matter with you, he began immediately to prescribe medicine, with no apparent concern for knowing you or the situation that had brought you to his office. Surely you would turn to another doctor the next time!

Well, that's the way we've treated the Indians in our neighborhoods. We are surrounded by people who would love to pour out the burdens of their hearts to someone. But we all look so busy — too busy to listen. And we all seem so cocksure, as though we already know the language of the Indian.

We are like the American tourist trying to make

her wants known to a shopkeeper in a foreign city. Amazed to discover that he does not seem to comprehend her English, the tourist repeats her demand, more loudly than before. After doing this several times, she turns in disgust to her traveling companion and says, "Wouldn't you think that if a person spoke slowly and plainly enough, *anybody* could understand English?"

We laugh at her provincialism. But our own efforts to win Indians without learning the language of their hearts is just as laughable and infinitely more tragic. It is a cheap sort of witnessing and a very ineffective sort of evangelism that tries to reach an Indian without learning his language.

In all the present-day discussions of the gift of tongues, where are those who will cry out to God for the ability to speak His truth the way the apostles did it on the Day of Pentecost, when they uttered the Good News and men heard it in their own languages? Do we know how much we need that ability today?

God will help us learn the language of our neighborhood Indians so that we may speak His truth to them on their wave length. But He will do it only if we are willing to listen to those whom we want to reach. When we have done that, we have every right to ask Him to help us, supernaturally, to leap over the linguistic barrier to reach them.

One day I was scheduled to speak at a luncheon meeting at the California Institute of Technology. As I sat with those brilliant men, most of them graduate students, I was overwhelmed by my own inadequacy for the task. It seemed as though intellectual electricity was crackling all around me in their conversation, and I never felt so ignorant in my life.

Almost in despair I cried out to God for His help. I knew I could not speak to them on their scientific level, but I believed it might be possible to help them know my Savior better if I listened carefully to that which seemed to concern them and if, above all else, I had the help of the Lord to bridge the gap.

God heard my prayer and answered. I was kept from babbling words that might seem intelligible to my own ears while sounding like a strange language to theirs. To the glory of God, I can say that some "Indians" heard the Gospel that day — in their own tongue, as they need to hear it.

It is never easy to overcome the linguistic barrier, but it is possible if we are aware the barrier exists and if, crying out to God for help, we take the pains to learn the language of the man we want to reach. Our witnessing is not really witnessing unless it is on the wavelength of those to whom we speak and in a language to which their hearts can respond.

On Bridging the Cultural Gap

Let's sum it up. There are Indians in your neighborhood: people utterly untouched by the Gospel, whom no Christian is making any effort to reach with the Good News. Moreover, it's hard to reach these Indians — hard, but not impossible. There are formidable barriers in the way, like geography and language; but by the power of God and our dedication to the task, these barriers can be overcome.

There is one other obstacle in the way, more difficult than either of the other two we have looked at. Indians, we discover, are different from us, not just because they live at a distance from us and speak a different language from ours, but because they come from a different culture.

This means that for generations all their patterns of thought, all their concepts, all their philosophy of life and action have been formed along different lines from ours: They are different from us, in the most fundamental and far-reaching ways; as a result an awesome gap lies between them and us.

A missionary going into any foreign culture soon learns this is one of the greatest problems he contends with. Long after he has learned the language of the people he continues to be very conscious that in some ways he lives in a different world from theirs. These whom he has come to serve think differently, react differently, and look at almost every situation differently from the way he does.

A Latin American is *not* like an Anglo-Saxon in

spite of their common humanity. The differences in their cultural heritage have seen to that, and there is no easy way to bridge the chasm this has created. A man can spend his life trying to understand another culture; while he may have a measure of success in this endeavor, he will always be conscious that a gap remains.

That is what makes it so difficult to reach the Indians in our neighborhoods. The fact is, they simply do not think the way we do. In their worldly culture they have been taught that one has to put his own interests first; our insistence that God must come first, others second, and ourselves last seems utterly incomprehensible to them.

They have been conditioned by several factors to believe that the life heaping up the largest amount of this world's goods is the most successful. Our claims that a man's life consists not in the abundance of things that he possesses sounds to them like pious double-talk which no sensible person would believe.

Our "Indian" friends come from a culture which insists that "you only go around once" and therefore you had better get everything you can — for yourself — while you have a chance. Our assertion that this life is only the beginning — and therefore a man ought to live with eternity's values in view appears to them to be the worst form of wishful thinking. They see this as a kind of forlorn idea that, since things haven't gone too well for us here and now, we'll convince ourselves they'll be better in some future life. To the Indian this sounds like errant nonsense.

I could multiply examples, but you have long since become aware that the difference between us and the Indians in our neighborhoods is not just geographical or linguistic. It is much more basic than that. It is cultural, and the gap is wide. How, then, will it be bridged? Can it be bridged? The answer to the latter question is "Yes — but not easily!" If we are serious about wanting to reach the Indians, the question of "How?" will occupy us for the rest of our lives.

Are you now waiting for me to give you a formula, a scheme, a surefire answer to this problem? Sorry, I don't have one. I don't know anyone who does. But I have seen this barrier overcome, and thus I am convinced it can be done.

This obstacle is most likely to be conquered, it seems to me, by the person who realizes the huge dimensions of the problem and who turns in utter helplessness to God for the answers no human wisdom can provide. Let me tell you how it worked out in one case.

It was a sense of desperation that drove three friends of mine to prayer. They are successful Christian businessmen — successful in the worldly sense of that term, and leaders in the Christian community as well. Their friends noted their zeal for the Lord, the outspokenness of their Christian witness, and their evident love for their fellowmen. But these three were terribly troubled in their hearts.

Each one felt that, for all his Christian activity, he was not getting through to the ones he most wanted to reach. The "Indians" were elusive, unreceptive, and my friends had the uneasy feeling that it was not the Indians' fault. They were very much aware that they were of one culture and the Indians were of another, and nothing was bridging the gap.

So they decided to get together at 6:30 A.M. once a week to talk to the Lord about their problem. These were no routine prayer meetings; they were times of grappling with the Lord over what seemed to them an almost insoluble problem, the culture-chasm which stood between them and the Indians whom they so much wanted to win for Christ.

The Lord heard their prayers and answered — not by giving them a formula, but by keeping them constantly aware of the problem and dependent upon Him for the solution.

One day, for example, having confessed to God the barrenness of their own lives and their need for help in reaching people of another culture, they went their separate ways to work. One of them stopped for lunch at a diner he often visited. He had no sooner sat down at the counter than the proprietor, a man whom he had witnessed to for years, apparently without effect, brought a cup of coffee and sat down on the next stool.

The two men, sitting close to each other but living in different worlds, began to discuss the usual harmless topics: the weather, sports, other similar subjects little affected by cultural differences. The innocuous conversation was suddenly interrupted when the diner's proprietor turned to my friend and blurted out, "Larry, there's something I've wanted to say to you for a long time, and today I'm going to say it! I have been watching you closely for fifteen years now, and there is something about the quality of your life that is different — and better — than anything I've ever known. Now tell me how I can have it."

Wisely, my friend didn't jump down his throat or embarrass him before his customers. Instead he quietly asked, "Are you sure you want to know?" When the other man insisted it was of utmost importance to him, my friend communicated the Gospel, from one diner stool to another and across a tremendous cultural gap, to an "Indian" who had never heard it before.

What does my story prove? Nothing, I suppose, if you are looking for a method to bridge the cultural gap. But it does say this to us about reaching the Indians who live simultaneously in our neighborhoods and in another world: when a Christian is conscious of the awesome nature of the gap, and when he cries out to God of his utter inadequacy to overcome this obstacle, the Lord moves in and does the impossible. The chasm is bridged, communication is established, Christ is made known to one who has lived in darkness.

Do you believe it? Would you like to prove it in your own life? God is not looking for experienced Indian-hunters. Instead He seeks those whom He can fill with love for the Indians in their neighborhoods, those who will depend on Him to overcome the geographic, linguistic, and cultural barriers that have so isolated them from these for whom Christ died.

If we make ourselves available to Him on that basis, the Indians in our neighborhoods can be reached!

Spiritual Gluttons

Spiritual Gluttons

My story is half biblical, half imaginary. I don't ask you to believe the imaginary part, but it gives food for thought.

It has been a long day. A crowd numbering in the thousands has listened for hours with rapt attention to the teacher. Now, as the shadows gather, they are hungry. But He knows they are hungry, even before the thought occurs to them. And He is determined to do something about it.

He has in His hands a few small loaves and some fish. He gives thanks for the humble repast, breaks the food into bits, and gives it to His disciples to distribute to the multitude, apparently convinced that there will be enough for everyone in the huge throng.

That part of the story is familiar to all of us. Next we move into the realm of the imagination, with no obligation to believe, only to listen: in the hope of learning about our well-fed selves and a hungry world.

As the disciples take the bits of bread and fish into their hands, they are suddenly conscious of how very hungry they are. They take everything the Lord has given them and, forgetting the crowd, they satisfy their own hunger with the food Christ has so bountifully provided. Some of them go back for a second helping, which the Lord graciously makes available to them. And a few gluttonous ones come back for still more — and get it.

They are all full — "stuffed," we would call it. So they sit down on the ground in a small circle and begin to talk piously about how good the Lord has been to them.

"Did you ever taste such good bread and fish?" asks one, and the prompt reply of another is, "No, I never did — but it's just like our Lord; He always provides the best."

A number of disciples nod their heads in agreement. Another speaks up, "Yes, and did you notice? It was a *miracle!* All He had was a little boy's lunch, and He fed all twelve of us with it. There is even some left over."

The rest acknowledge the wonder of it all and how great must be the power of One who can feed twelve people with what originally was meant for only one.

One disciple comments that, while the food is indeed wonderful, the really great thing is the fellowship they have enjoyed with one another and with the Lord. No one is disposed to argue against this point, and they all agree when a disciple says, "You know, we really ought to do this every week. We could come together every seven days and have a wonderful time of Christian fellowship, with the Lord providing the food."

This last suggestion prompts a response from a disciple who hasn't been heard from until now. "Well," he says, with an attempt at modesty, "you men know that I have a bit of a gift for poetry. If we're going to meet weekly, I'll compose a song — a sort of theme chorus — that we can sing each time. It will tell how great our Lord is, how good is the food which He provides, and what a good time we have together."

His offer is quickly accepted, and this encourages another disciple to say, "Well, I haven't any poetic gift, but I do seem to possess a knack for arranging things, and if you'd like, I'll be glad to be chairman of the program committee. With your help, I'll draw up a different program for each week, so we never get bored at our meetings."

All agree a program committee is a good idea and breathe a sigh of relief that someone is willing to head it up. One man is a bit ill at ease, and he finally speaks up. "It's wonderful to be so well fed, but we mustn't forget that probably in other parts of the world some people are hungry. Once a year we ought to think about these hungry ones."

This sparks an animated discussion in which almost all of the disciples take part. Their conclusions: they will have an annual series of meetings to inform themselves about the plight of hungry people; they'll even invite some special speakers on such occasions — those who have been feeding the hungry in other places and who will report on their work; they may hear testimonies from some who were starving but now are well fed; and they'll have special decorations — perhaps the flags of countries where it is reported there is much hunger.

One point elicits more discussion and gets more support than all the others: on such occasions, after they've had a feast themselves, they'll send whatever is leftover to hungry people in other lands.

By now it is almost dark, and the group suddenly decides it's time to go home. As they disappear down the path, fragments of their conversation drift back to us. "I can hardly wait until next week," says one. An excited babble indicates common consent. "Our Lord is surely good to us — such good food and such good fellowship!" cries another. Almost spontaneously the group joins in singing, "Praise God from whom all blessings flow. . . ." It has indeed been a memorable day; they have enjoyed it thoroughly and have discharged their duty, they think, by thanking God for such a wonderful time.

Meanwhile, five thousand men plus women and children are still hungry. There is no food for them tonight. It's not because Christ didn't provide enough, but because some spiritual gluttons got to it first, never asking why they had so much, never really seeing the hunger of the others.

Might this be a parable for our own day?

Beyond Bafflement

Many Christians seem baffled by the times in which we live. They recognize that everything we hold dear is not merely under scrutiny, but even under attack. Within the Church and outside of it, a battle goes on, and nothing, however sacred, seems to escape the ravages of the conflict.

There are many persons — some of them in ecclesiastical high places — who blatantly announce that the "old, old story" of the Gospel may be beautiful but has no relevance for our day.

The church is being fired on, too. It would seem that one way to hit the best-seller lists is to write a book exposing the alleged weaknesses and inconsistencies of this venerable institution. Recent years have seen books like *The Suburban Captivity of the Churches* and *The Comfortable Pew* attracting wide attention to their uninhibited criticisms of the organized church.

Nor is the missionary enterprise outside the range of fire. It faces a host of unsympathetic critics who have decided that any attempt to win men and nations to faith in Jesus Christ is hostile and plainly out-of-date.

What should we do in a time like this? How should we face such all-out onslaughts? The answers are not easy to come by. Many Christians admit they are baffled that evil seems totally unrestrained. The enemies of the Christian faith seem so relentless in their attacks!

But bafflement is the prelude to discouragement, and discouragement often issues in spiritual paralysis. In this situation we need to ask ourselves, "What does God expect us to be doing in a time like this?" Without pretending to answer that question exhaustively, let me suggest three things:

1. We ought to listen to the criticisms — even from the enemies of the Gospel — and examine ourselves and the household of God in the light of them. Unfortunately not all their charges are false; we are vulnerable to some. We haven't always represented our Savior and His Gospel suitably, and we ought to be honest enough to admit it. It is much more appropriate, on occasion, to confess our failures than to try to make a blanket defense of everything we've said and done in the name of Christ. We have much to learn of what it really means to serve God in a day like this, and He will use even the accusations of our enemies to teach us.

2. We ought to answer, in a manner worthy of Christ, the attacks of godless men against the Christian faith. The charges that the Bible is full of myth, hence utterly unreliable, should be met by fresh, scholarly demonstrations of the absolute trustworthiness of God's Word rather than by ranting attacks on the accusers. The errors of false teachers need to be exposed. God will give us, if we see the need and ask Him, evangelical leaders who are more than a match for the deniers and diluters of the faith.

3. We ought to get on with the job. In a way, this must take priority over all else. We dare not be sidetracked into defending ourselves, and in the final analysis the Gospel needs no defense. Indeed, Christ asks not that we defend it but that we proclaim it — fearlessly, with absolute confidence in its power. He can be counted on to vindicate Himself when His truth is faithfully presented.

After all, the most effective argument for the biblical message remains transformed lives. Men who are truly "saved" — saved for heaven but also from self-centeredness, shortsightedness, and lack of concern for others — are the best evidence that the Gospel's power has not waned.

Moreover, the work of the church will be advanced less by the clever answers we give to its critics than by our giving ourselves completely to evangelizing the nations and the man next door.

We dare not allow ourselves to be paralyzed with fear when our Lord and His church come under attack. Bafflement in such a situation is a terribly expensive luxury. There is a worldwide need to be met, a job to be done, a Savior to be honored. The ultimate evidence of our absolute confidence in Him is not found in our arguments on His behalf but in our unceasing determination to proclaim Him and His Gospel.

Martin Luther had moved, by the grace of God, beyond bafflement when he wrote:

> And tho' this world, with devils filled,
> Should threaten to undo us;
> We will not fear, for God hath willed
> His truth to triumph through us.

Let's Be Careful With Labels!

When labels are honest and accurate, they help tremendously. They give us confidence that when we pick a package off the supermarket shelf, we may be sure what we're getting. When we reach into the medicine cabinet and read the label on the bottle carefully, we know we have the needed remedy and not some poison that will do us irreparable damage.

But what if labels are inaccurate? What if they don't tell the truth? What happens when we can't trust them? Under these circumstances, the possibilities are terrifying to contemplate: misrepresentation, disappointment, fraud, perhaps even death. As a result, "truth in packaging" has in recent times become a concern of our federal government.

There's a warning here for us. Truth in packaging is terribly important in the religious realm, where we're often quick to pin labels on persons and organizations.

The trouble is that we're not always careful for the accuracy of the labels we use. Such carelessness is at best unfortunate; at worst, it is spiritually disastrous.

The problem with many of our labels is that they are just too general. They fail to consider sufficiently the complexity of the product described.

In some circles, for example, to label a person a member of one of the old-line denominations seems enough to condemn him. Over-pious people sometimes express their judgment of a fellow Christian by pinning a denominational label on him and then asking, "Can any good come out of that group?" It's as though there were some kind of standard product known as "Presbyterian" or "Episcopalian" or "Methodist," with the consequence that to identify a person with one of these is to describe him spiritually.

Such a misuse of labels overlooks the fact that there are all sorts of people within these groups, spiritually speaking, just as there are in nondenominational churches. Consequently we don't really say anything of a person's spiritual state when we merely identify him with some man-made organization. To praise a person or to condemn him just because such a label can be affixed to him is evidence of a superficial judgment indeed — the kind of judgment Christ surely condemns.

There was a day when to say a person was a Roman Catholic seemed to label him fairly accurately. We pictured immediately someone in an utterly unscriptural system, who by his very participation in it showed that he must be blind to the basic biblical truths which made the Reformation necessary; he must therefore be living in spiritual darkness.

If the business of labeling were ever that simple, it is no longer. Not because the church of Rome has changed so much, but because so many of her members now have serious doubts about her doctrines, search the Scriptures for valid answers, and respond to gracious influences that the Spirit of God brings to bear on them.

In this situation, we are not called either to defend the Catholic Church or to overlook her grievous errors. But we do need to realize, in a new way, that when we speak of a person as a Roman Catholic we have used a very general label and therefore not a very descriptive one. Calling him a Catholic says little about his spiritual conditon.

Sometimes the term "ecumenical" is used as though it accurately portrayed the theological stance and the spiritual state of the person to whom we have attached the label. There are at least two things wrong with this kind of label-pinning.

First, we need to remember that a concern for the

visible unity of the Body of Christ is thoroughly grounded in the Scriptures. It is not necessarily connected with the "ecumenical movement" or any other organizational effort to promote that unity.

Second, using the term "ecumenical" as a sort of poison-warning overlooks the fact that many true believers are related directly or indirectly to ecumenically oriented groups. Their involvement may be by decision or by default, but it indicates nothing about their spiritual condition.

Saying this does not defend the ecumenical movement or ignore its deficiencies. But we are obligated by the Scriptures to recognize our relationship to God's born-again people wherever they are found — and to be scrupulously honest and accurate if we start pinning labels on them. Our relationship to other believers is based on our common union by faith to Jesus Christ — and not on the organizations to which we belong or the movements to which we give allegiance.

To downgrade a person by calling him "ecumenical" is both unfair and unjust and, consequently, unworthy of a Christian — doubly so if the person we thus label is a member of the redeemed family of God.

Labels are convenient, and there will always be a need for them. But let them be honest labels. Let our categories be scriptural ones, not humanly devised labels which divide Christians as Christ never meant us to be divided.

We could use more of the spirit of Henry Martyn, great evangelical missionary of another age, who wrote, "I am more than ever anxious to know no man after his sect as an Independent, Presbyterian, Methodist, or Baptist. . . . Let us love him exceedingly in whom we see much of Christ though his opinions are contrary to our own. So we shall know we are passed from death unto life, and sectarian quarrels will cease."

Let's be careful with labels — for Jesus' sake!

The Word Makes the Difference

It was one of those days when the teacher of the class thought the bell would never ring to terminate his agony. I was the teacher, and my class was a group of young students preparing themselves for the Lord's service at the Latin American Biblical Seminary in San Jose, Costa Rica.

Somehow everything had gone wrong in the class that day, and I was deeply conscious of my inadequacy, linguistically and otherwise, to teach this group. I wanted the bell to ring — and even more, I wanted to resign from the faculty. In a silent but heartfelt prayer I told the Lord that if He would get me through this one class I would never teach again. It seemed plainly unfair that a group of students as competent as these should be subjected to me!

When at last I heard the bell's welcome sound, I gathered up my Bible and notebook and hurried in humiliation to the door of the classroom. To my surprise I found my way barred by the members of the class, who were gathered in a small semicircle with their backs to the door.

A student from Colombia, apparently the appointed spokesman for the group, said, "Don Horacio, we have a question we'd like to ask you." I felt I'd scream if I had to answer one more question! But there was no escape, so I encouraged him to speak up.

I wasn't prepared for what he said:

"Don Horacio, three times a week you've been showing us how to take a paragraph of God's Word, find its meaning for our lives, and then organize its essence so that we can communicate it to others. But three times a week isn't enough, and we want to know if you can give us an extra class each week so that we can learn even more about how to dig into the Scriptures."

Bewildered, I sparred for time. "Suppose we did meet four times a week," I replied, "what would we do in the extra class?" (The question was very practical, as far as I was concerned; I was having a hard time preparing for three classes a week!)

He saw no problem in the situation. "That's easy," he answered. "Let's just do more of what we're already doing: taking paragraphs of Scripture, observing them closely, noting their meaning, finding their application to ourselves and others, and then discovering ways of communicating these truths to those who need them."

I forgot all about my vow to the Lord never to teach again! We met four times a week after that. There was never any need to check attendance in the extra class — they were so eager, so hungry, so desiring to understand the Scriptures.

When people ask me why the Lord has so many choice and fruitful servants among the national believers in Latin America, I tell the story of my seminary class — and of the difference a hunger for the Word makes. Those students are scattered all over Latin America today to serve the Lord. Their usefulness for Him is in direct proportion to their continued immersion in the Word of God.

Does that say anything to you?

A Lower Standard of Living

A missionary returning to his homeland after being away a few years inevitably experiences culture shock in reverse. He is immediately and almost overwhelmingly impressed with the rise in America's standard of living during the period of his absence. This contrasts not only with the comparative poverty of "the mission field," but also with the homeland itself as he knew it a few years earlier.

People seem to have more conveniences, multiplied gadgets, finer cars, and a number of luxuries they hadn't dreamed of when he left for foreign shores.

Now, no one — not even the returned missionary — would say there is anything inherently sinful about this marked improvement in living conditions. Nor would he begrudge to anyone the acquisition of creature comforts never previously enjoyed. If money is available to make life more comfortable and to render the strains of daily existence more bearable, why shouldn't it be spent for these things?

And if Christians, swept along by the pressures of advertising and the rising tide of economic progress, seem to need more things to satisfy their earthly necessities, who is to condemn them? Not their fellow Christians, surely, since most find themselves subjected to the same pressures. And not the returned missionary, who recognizes that his negative reaction to this situation may well be inspired by jealousy!

Yet for most of us there is an occasional feeling of guilt and self-condemnation as we survey the abundance of things we possess. Perhaps it is because we have always proclaimed, as part of our Christian message, that life doesn't really consist in the possession of these things and that they can never satisfy the needs of the human heart. We wonder if our actions don't belie our words. Things do seem pretty important to us; not really essential, of course, but more important than they used to be, at any rate.

Our qualms of conscience may have a deeper root. They may spring from our inability to forget One who possessed everything — all the glory of heaven, in a fullness we cannot even imagine — and who gave it all up, for us.

Paul tells about it in the second chapter of his letter to the Philippians. He calls us to behold our Lord, laying aside all that is rightly His and humbling Himself. Here is the eternal Son of God, choosing a lower standard of living than He had ever known, voluntarily relinquishing all that He had, to become the Savior of men.

Our usual method of handling this passage is to treat it like a theological football. The scholars kick it back and forth, making a game of their debates about the extent of Christ's self-humiliation. Such arguments may have some academic justification, but when Paul wrote these words he had a much more practical aim. He wanted us to see our Lord gladly letting go of all that was His, joyfully choosing our lowly estate, in order to redeem us.

But Paul didn't mean we should stop there, merely admiring what Christ did. Instead, he says, "Let this mind be in you. . . ." And that's where our trouble comes. We want to be like Christ, but not too much like Him. We want to prove that He meets our every need, but we don't want to let go of those things on which we depend so heavily.

We want to support the work of God, provided it doesn't interfere too much with our standard of living. We want to see souls saved and the Gospel of

Christ taken to the ends of the earth — if this may be accomplished without altering greatly our own plans and restricting unduly our way of life.

But God simply won't let us be comfortable with that outlook. He is determined that His children demonstrate that their joy does not depend on possession of things — not even legitimate things. He knows discipleship means death — death to self, in its more attractive manifestations as well as more loathsome forms. He insists no man can take up his cross without letting go of whatever else he is carrying.

The father is satisfied with nothing less than seeing in His children the very mind of His own dear Son, who thought nothing was worth holding onto when the salvation of the world was at stake.

That's why so many Christians are not enjoying their higher standard of living as much as they had expected to. The problem is, there is always at hand a disturbing Figure who saved them by choosing a lower standard of life; He calls them to the same kind of self-renunciation, that the Gospel might go to the ends of the earth and that men might be saved in every tribe and nation.

You see, the admonition to "let this mind be in you, which was also in Christ Jesus" is not just a beautiful verse, not just a lovely text around which a preacher can build a sermon. Instead it is a clarion call to a lower standard of living — for Jesus' sake and for the sake of a needy world. Have we really heard *that* call?

"Doesn't Anyone Care?"

It was six in the morning when my telephone rang. The voice on the other end urged me to go at once to the apartment of a member of our church. I didn't get all the details, but it was apparent a tragedy had occurred. I hurriedly got dressed and made my way across town.

A middle-aged woman, a sincere Christian abandoned by her husband years before, ushered me into her living room. From the day her husband left, her life had been wrapped up in her only child. He grew into a young man who had returned from service in the Navy just a few days before I received this phone call.

Now the lifeless body of this son was stretched out on the floor in the next room. He had been cleaning a rifle, very early in the morning, when it accidentally discharged — and the woman who had no husband now had no son either.

As we sat together in the darkened living room, I kept praying that somehow, amid her sadness, she would see a glimpse of light. Abruptly she got up from her chair, went to the window, and looked out on the crowds of people hurrying on their way to their jobs. Then she gave an anguished cry, "Doesn't anybody care? My boy is dead — and the world just goes on as usual!"

I think I know how she felt. It seemed to her that the whole world ought to share her grief, but no one was paying attention. There was inexpressible heartbreak behind her question: "Doesn't anybody care?"

I thought of a man who must have felt that way centuries earlier. His battered, broken body lay beside the road that went down from Jerusalem to Jericho, and he kept hoping someone would bring help. The road was lonely, but occasionally someone came along; momentarily the wounded man saw the possibility of rescue. Yet one person after another took a quick look at him and then passed by on the other side. It looked as though no one cared.

It must look that way to many people today. They have burdens they don't know how to bear, and no one seems interested in helping them. They long for sympathy, for counsel, for even a smile — and no one gives it.

I stood one day amid indescribable slums on the outskirts of Lima, Peru. I saw people condemned to live like animals in a wretchedness of poverty that was neither their choice nor their fault. I felt ashamed of my clothing — nothing special by stateside standards, but regal compared with their rags. I remembered my home, modest but comfortable, and I compared it with these shacks of mud, tar paper, cardboard, and tin. It seemed to me that in the wondering eyes of these underfed people I read the same question the bereaved woman had asked: "Doesn't anyone care?"

On another occasion I watched the students on a large university campus in Latin America. More than 100,000 young people are enrolled in that one institution, and in some ways they are a very special group. But they are hungry — spiritually hungry — without knowing what they hunger for. Like their North American counterparts, they are trying everything in a frantic but futile attempt to satisfy the gnawings inside. I knew there was little likelihood of their being fed; too few Christians were even thinking about them, let alone doing something to meet their spiritual need. The students didn't voice the question, but they had every right to: "Doesn't anyone care?"

In most cases, the answer to that question is the

same today as it was long ago, when that bleeding hulk lay by the side of the Jericho road, hoping against hope for help. Seemingly the answer has to be, "No, no one cares — not even the religious people like the priest and the Levite!"

Now it's all too easy to throw stones at those who hurried past the helpless form by the roadside. It gives us a smug sense of self-satisfaction whenever we find someone who has even less compassion than we have. The fact is, the priest and the Levite were probably no worse than most of us, who have found more refined ways of telling men that we see their plight but do nothing about it.

You see, the real question is not, "Why didn't the priest and Levite do something?" but rather, "Why don't we — in the face of all sorts of tragic situations — why don't we do something?"

Maybe the priest and Levite thought they were too busy to stop. That's the excuse we so frequently use. They were on their way about their religious duties; time was short; they just couldn't afford to pause to help the victim. If this was their problem, the essence of it was that they were putting things before people; meetings before men; the needs of their schedule before the hurt of humanity. Can't you imagine how Christ would have dealt with that kind of thinking? We remember how He refused to consider a needy woman an interruption, even though He was hurrying on His way to meet another's need. For Christ, needy people were never "interruptions." Someone had to care, and He would even if no one else did.

If we are to be like Christ, we will have to make place in our busy schedules for needy people. Someone *has* to care!

Perhaps the priest and the Levite weren't moved because the suffering man wasn't of their kind. If only he had been a fellow priest, another Levite —

well, that would have been different! One reason why the cause of missions languishes in many a so-called evangelical church today is that we hesitate to help those who are not "our kind." If only they looked like us, thought like us, responded the way we expected them to! But the whole point of Christ's parable of the good Samaritan is that all a man needs to commend him to our compassion is his need — not his looks, not his economic status, not his likeness to us. When will we ever learn?

Maybe the priest and Levite thought they would discharge their duty if they expressed a bit of sympathy or offered up a brief prayer. Isn't that a good thing to do? Of course it is — but it's not enough if you have it in your power to do more. To a helpless man beside the road, sympathy may seem a mockery; prayer, an exercise in futility; the gift of money, an empty thing — unless these gestures are accompanied by a helping hand and a binding up of wounds.

Some of us today appear to think that bewailing the condition of our world is a form of Christian service. We act as though it is enough to feel sorry about empty bellies or lost souls. We think we have done our spiritual duty when we pray for afflicted people. And all the while the suffering ones cry out, "Doesn't anyone care?"

But now and then a good Samaritan comes along — a person not too busy to stop, not too foreign to show compassion, who accompanies his good wishes by good works. Someone cares! You see, in the light of Christ's teaching here and in the light of need all around us today, a threefold response is called for if we really claim to be His followers.

In the first place, there must be a confession of sin. The fact is, none of us has cared as much about the needs of others as we should.

We stand condemned by the example of Christ and

by the unmet needs of men who still wonder whether anyone cares.

Second, a declaration of purpose is fitting. Let us say to our Lord and to needy men, "I mean to care — in a Christlike way!"

Finally, we may well utter a plea for guidance: "Lord, there is so much need; where do You want me to start?"

To all of needy humanity, everywhere, there must be an affirmative answer to the haunting question, "Doesn't anyone care?" The truth of the Gospel is that Christ cares. The demonstration of the Gospel comes when we care, too, and do something about it.

Marching Off the Map

Marching Off the Map

Marching Off the Map — that was Halford Luccock's intriguing title for his devotional commentary on the Book of Acts. Somehow, in this picturesque phrase, he captured the restless, unflagging drive of the early church.

The disciples must have been amazed to hear the risen Savior talk about their taking His Gospel to "Jerusalem . . . Judea . . . Samaria . . . the uttermost part of the earth." He held before them a staggering task; they were being thrust forth to places they couldn't even picture. He was calling them to march off the map.

In the ensuing months and years, they learned that this was not merely a geographical matter. To be sure, they were to move out to strange parts of the globe to make Christ known. But there was more to it than that. Christ would be taking them — and sometimes pushing them — beyond all the limits they had known, in the social, the intellectual, and the spiritual levels of their existence.

They would spend the rest of their lives marching off the neat little maps they had previously known.

Something of this sort is always involved in a living relationship with Christ. He calls us, not to tarry in the drab routine which too many of us have allowed our Christian lives to become, but rather to move out with Him beyond the frontiers — out where our carefully drawn, man-made maps won't serve us anymore.

Christ calls every one of us today — not just to a new location, not merely to some human organization, but to Himself and to areas which are still inadequately charted.

This is true geographically, even after nineteen centuries of missionary endeavor. There are still tiny tribes and mammoth cities which no one has sufficiently penetrated with the Gospel. Although pinpoints of light in countless places today replace the unrelieved darkness of a century ago, we cannot rest content so long as there are primeval forests and concrete jungles where the Good News is unknown. There is plenty of uncharted territory of this sort, and Christ still looks for those who will march off the map with Him.

But the problem isn't only geographical. Other levels of human existence remain uncharted, where no one has yet gone with an effective witness for Christ.

Take the revolution-ridden areas of earth, for example — vast territories where men struggle, often violently, for a more adequate level of subsistence and a sense of dignity and worth. Does the Gospel have anything to say to these unhappy people, in the context of their life-and-death strivings?

You would think not if you looked on the shelves of our evangelical libraries or listened to the sermons preached in affluent America! This is uncharted territory; someone needs to march off the map. God is calling those who believe His Word to seek new and fresh ways to relate His truth to the everyday efforts of men, so that even in a revolutionary era, when the oppressed battle for their very existence, His Gospel will have a fair hearing.

Have we really learned to use the mass media to communicate the Good News effectively? We've made some progress in this area, of course; but in a day when secular men take communication ever more seriously, we who are Christ's surely have some uncharted realms to explore. The maps of culture and communication which we have drawn up until now fail to take us far enough. Christ still calls men to march off the map for Him and with Him.

Only in recent times has the church begun to take seriously the task of reaching students around the world. God has blessed our efforts, but our maps have been too small. The big advance on the student world in the name of Christ is yet to come. No intelligent Christian may be satisfied with our present rate of progress. Thankful for past blessings, yet dissatisfied with the current situation, we are called by Christ to move, to march, to break across new frontiers where our old maps won't serve us, and to claim for Him untrodden areas on the campuses of the world.

Surely in these and in a host of other ways, God calls to His church today, insisting that in a new sense we will be Christ's disciples and go marching off the map.

"We Are Not Divided"

You don't hear "Onward, Christian Soldiers" very often in the churches these days. Perhaps this is because the military theme of the hymn doesn't appeal much to a nation that has seen more than enough of war.

It's even more likely that our problem is with the beautiful line, "We are not divided; All one body we." To sing these words lightly gives us no problem, but when we think about them, we feel a bit uneasy. Only in the most mystical of senses do we dare to claim we are not divided. We surely seem to be!

It isn't that we long for a super-organization of Christians or expect some sort of uniformity imposed from without to give us the unity we seek. The New Testament clearly teaches that God wills a fuller manifestation of our unity in Christ than we have yet experienced. Moreover, if we are at all serious about making Christ known throughout the world, we'll have to come to grips with the problem we have in trying to sing this great hymn with a straight face.

The issue is especially crucial on the mission field. There the enormity of the task and the bitterness of the spiritual conflict make it essential that we be able to proclaim with a measure of truth that "we are not divided."

It is not necessarily a matter of merging organizations —although that may be called for on occasion. The real question is whether evangelical mission boards will set themselves increasingly to finding new ways of working together in fulfilling our God-given task.

The picture is not totally dark. Latin America in

recent years has seen increasing cooperation among evangelical groups in the fields of evangelism, radio, and literature. For all such progress, we ought to give thanks to God. It's too late in the day for us who belong to the same Savior to be completely isolated from one another as we serve Him. We can't afford the luxury of undue competitiveness with each other in the work of the Lord today.

As we thank God for what has been done in this regard, we should continually seek new areas in which we may cooperate with individuals and groups who share our convictions of Christ and the Scriptures. Our bold declaration that we are not divided will then have a greater ring of truth than now.

There is another realm in which our unity in Christ must be manifested on the mission field. In times past our thinking has tended to put stress on the missionaries at one time, on the national believers at another. In one sense there is a valid distinction between the two groups; yet the basic and all-important truth is not the difference between them, but the fact that all are one in Jesus Christ.

For various reasons, there exists on many mission fields today a wide gulf between the mission and the national church, and consequently an undue stress on the distinctive features of each group. This cannot be pleasing to the Lord. He gave Himself, not only to break down the middle wall of partition between Jew and Gentile, but also to make all believers, of every race, more conscious of their relationship to one another in Christ than of their national and cultural differences.

We can thank God for progress along these lines, too, in our mission and in other groups; but we dare not be satisfied. We still have put too little meaning into our claim of oneness in Christ.

We are not divided. That claim may either be like

a hollow mockery or be a statement which becomes more of a glorious reality with the passing of time. There is no doubt about God's will in the matter, or about the demands of the job before us. Let us pray, then, in confidence that we may join with all who love Him in fulfilling the unfinished task; thus we will demonstrate to men and to angels that "we are not divided."

The End of Earth's Dark Night

Some nights seem as though they will never end. To the pain-wracked patient, tossing on his hospital bed, the coming of morning seems indefinitely postponed. The weary truck driver, pushing his rig hour after hour through the darkness, begins to wonder whether dawn will ever arrive.

The world into which Christ came seemed in the grip of an endless night. It was shrouded in an almost impenetrable darkness. Hardly anyone dared to hope that light would ever again break through. For God's chosen people especially, the night seemed interminable.

They knew, for one thing, the darkness of slavery. No chains bound them in a literal sense, but they were slaves nonetheless — of a hated occupying power who ground their land under the heel of its conquering legions. No Jew was really free while Rome dominated the world scene; deliverance from the galling yoke seemed only a wild dream with little hope of fulfillment. It was a long, dark night with apparently no glimmer of light to relieve the blackness.

Then Christ came, and though many did not realize it at the time, the night of slavery was drawing to its end. John's simple way of putting it tells the story: "The light shines in the darkness, and the darkness has not overcome it" (John 1:5, rsv).

Today men still find themselves slaves. Some nations are in bondage to tyrants with no relief on the horizon. Even in lands where slavery is outlawed, men find themselves captives to their passions, enslaved by their lusts, dominated by their appetites. Freedom is to them a mockery, for their souls are enslaved and they see no way of escape.

The first man I ever spoke to about Christ surprised me by his response. I was a high school student, helping in an open-air service and terribly conscious that I was expected to seek out someone listening to our message and ask him about his relationship to the Lord Jesus. I observed a man who seemed to show some interest in our meeting but, aware of my youth and inexperience, I was afraid to approach him.

Finally I could stand the Holy Spirit's pressure no longer, and I blurted out my question, "Sir, do you know the Lord Jesus Christ?" I'll never forget his answer. He grabbed me by the arm and replied to my question with a query of his own: "Young man, can your Christ help someone who's made a mess out of life the way I have?"

In a torrent of words he poured out his story, a tale of unbridled appetites, of consequent loss of family and friends, of remorse, of resolutions to do better, and of consistent failure to do so. It was the cry of a man who knew himself to be in the darkness of bondage, who had begun to fear this long night would never end.

My word to him — and to many like him through the years since then — was the message of a Light which came into the world long ago, a Light which the darkness has never been able to overcome.

When that Light entered the world, many in Israel learned that the end of their long night of slavery was at hand. Rome wasn't overthrown immediately, of course; but followers of Him who was the Light found freedom for their souls, grace to endure the seemingly unbearable Roman yoke for a time, and a sweet confidence that God, not Caesar, would have the last word. That's the way it worked out. For many an Israelite, when the Light came into his life his slavery ended.

So it has been for slaves in our own time. The struggle to be free from ourselves and our circumstances is never easy. But the darkness of slavery cannot remain where the light of Christ is; the night in man's soul ends when he welcomes the Savior into his heart.

For some, the long night is not one of slavery but of frustrated hopes. The Israelites knew all about that, too. Through the centuries they counted on their armies to save them; they relied on their kings to bring them victory. They set their hope on military might only to find that it betrayed them. When God sent the prophets to His people, these rugged men seemed a new source of hope. But the prophets came and went, and the sense of futility and frustration remained.

Today the darkness which grips the world likewise consists of frustrated hopes. The endless round of their meaningless existence torments people. Surely, they think, life was meant to be something better than this. They have heard a report that man was made in the image of God, but they see very little in their friends and neighbors — or in themselves — which seems to show any relationship to the divine. And what, they want to know, has happened to that brave, new world which men have promised?

Is our civilization at long last going out, as T. S. Eliot put it, "not with a bang, but a whimper"? And if so, what has happened to all the high hopes man has held for himself and his race down through the centuries?

This is darkness indeed, and there is no remedy for it—except Light, the kind of light that Christ brought into the world. When Christ came, He brought a new dimension to our lives by showing us how, through trusting in Him, we might become sons of God. He called men to follow Him and serve needy souls.

Suddenly there was hope, because their lives had been invested with a new dignity. Life had a purpose now; there was a point to it all. God was working in His world and in each life committed to Him — and so there was hope.

The light was shining in the darkness, and the darkness could not overcome it. The night was over!

But what darkness has been brought into men's hearts by dead religion! This was the kind of thing which characterized the long, dark night that enveloped the world into which Christ came. Religion there was plenty of: lovely forms, beautiful buildings, incense from countless altars. But it was all so *dead*— so sterile — so empty! Men were tired of going through the motions, playing religious games. Those empty rituals have never satisfied the deep needs of men's hearts. The husks that the swine eat are a poor substitute for the delicacies of the Father's table; the most debased of humans somehow knows there is a difference between the diet of pigs and the banquets of rich men's sons.

Yet we go on playing our games and trying to subsist on husks. And we wonder why it seems as though the night will never end.

But Christ is the end of this night, too. When the Light shines, the darkness has to disappear — even the darkness of empty, meaningless forms and ceremonies, of religion without life. He is not only Light but also Life, and He transforms the emptiness of a dead religion into the fullness of fellowship with God. The believing Israelites learned to talk, not of a religion, but of a Person ("We beheld His glory!" "We handled the Word of life!").

A young philosophy student recently asked his professor, "Can it be that it is really possible to know God?" Thankfully, the professor knew God's own answer to that question. He was able not only to respond with a resounding affirmative but also to point the student to Christ — the Light who has forever banished the darkness of empty religion.

There are still plenty of pockets of darkness in this old world. And there are still multitudes of people who don't know that the Light has come and that the darkness is on its way out because there is no such thing as peaceful coexistence between Light and darkness. But we who are Christians have seen the Savior put an end to our night. On the authority of His Word and of the experience of great multitudes who have seen Him banish their darkness, we invite men everywhere to find in Him the end of their slavery, their frustrated hopes, their dead religion.

All the while, the words of the hymn writer become our fervent prayer to Him:

> O Jesus, ever with us stay,
> Make all our moments calm and bright;
> Chase the dark night of sin away,
> Shed o'er the world Thy holy light.

Two Kinds of Witness

Some of the words we use most frequently we understand least. Take "witness" — a popular word in Christian circles these days. Indeed, we use it so often it seems to have lost meaning — like a coin that has passed through so many hands its original image is almost obliterated. We have spoken so much of witness that we have lost any clear-cut idea as to what it means. And we often substitute a very narrow and limited concept for the word's meaning, in both biblical and current terms.

A court of law has at least two kinds of witness: verbal and nonverbal. In the first sense, witness is something spoken or written. A few years ago I was unexpectedly summoned from California to be a witness in a trial taking place in Kansas City. I had no choice in the matter; once the authorities learned I had had some contact with the defendant when he had traveled through Costa Rica a few years earlier, they demanded that I come to the courtroom and tell what I knew about him. By even a limited contact with him I was qualified to speak as a witness.

This must have been the kind of thing our Lord had in mind when, just before His ascension, He told His disciples that they would receive power and be witnesses to Him. These men had many limitations, but they had been with Jesus. They had known Him first hand — as most of the rest of the world had not. In this realm at least, they were experts, and He called them to share their knowledge with a world woefully ignorant of Him.

So it is with us. If we know anything of Christ —

anything of His power to forgive, to transform, to strengthen, to sustain — we know something that most men have yet to learn. If we have experienced the power of prayer or the joy of the Lord, we are qualified to be witnesses to these things. We may never be preachers or teachers or missionaries in the technical, limited sense, but we can be witnesses.

Bishop Stephen Neill estimates that one-third of the world has never heard the name of Christ and another third has not heard enough to make an intelligent decision concerning Him. If this be so, we are surrounded with opportunities for witness; Christ expects us to take advantage of them.

But there is another kind of witness: nonverbal. We Christians are in danger of giving too little thought to this kind of testimony. In my brief experience in the courtroom I learned that judge, lawyers, and jury are interested in more than what the witness says. They try, by every means at their command, to evaluate the witness himself — to know whether his character confirms or denies his testimony. The witness may give himself away by a careless word, a thoughtless gesture, or some other act that contradicts what he has said. His testimony is not only what he says but what he is.

This is the very thing that made the witness of the early church so effective. As these Christians testified everywhere to the risen Christ, an unbelieving world scrutinized their lives with great care. They discovered that these people were brave, filled with courage that could not be explained apart from Christ. They noted that these Christians genuinely loved their fellowmen in a way unknown among the heathen. It was evident that the believers were morally pure in an age when this kind of thing was rare, if not humanly impossible to achieve.

Thus an unbelieving world was faced with the issues

of Christ and eternal life — not just by the words that proclaimed Him but by the lives that manifested Him. Verbal testimony and nonverbal agreed, and many were moved and converted by the witness.

We need, at this time, to stress both kinds of witness. Too often the orthodoxy of our doctrine is not confirmed by consistency in our lives. Our words of witness sound hollow and unconvincing, because our lives do not tell the same story. The world needs to hear about Jesus, but it needs even more to see Him. The witness of words and the witness of works, when they concur, offer a powerful argument for the truth of the Gospel. A witness without words or a witness without works is not the witness to which God calls us.

When Ignorance is Costly

Ignorance is sometimes harmless. I have met people in the interior of Latin America who know little or nothing about the mysteries of space travel or television or expressways. Yet they know Christ in a vital way, and their lives have been transformed by Him. In the light of their knowledge of that which is truly important, I'm not inclined to feel sorry about their ignorance of lesser things.

But some ignorance is basically tragic and terribly costly. When I saw Indians in Guatemala consult with a witch doctor, then prostrate themselves before pagan deities, only to turn a few minutes later to offer the same kind of worship to the Virgin Mary, I felt I beheld an ignorance of the true God which could only be called costly and tragic.

It was of this kind of ignorance that our Lord Jesus spoke wistfully to the woman at Samaria's well: "If thou knewest the gift of God, and who it is that saith unto thee, Give me to drink . . ." (John 4:10). Here was tragedy indeed. Whatever else this woman knew, she was ignorant that God was offering to supply her greatest need and that she was standing in the very presence of the One who was the Father's provision for her. She didn't know the gift, and she didn't know the Giver. Her ignorance was not a trivial kind; it was costly beyond words.

Christ says the same thing to non-Christians today. If only they knew what God offers them — but they don't! Perhaps they have recieved a distorted picture of the Christian life, and it consequently appears to them to be joyless and negative. Perhaps they have thought of eternal life in purely quantitative terms — an endless existence in a totally unattractive place. No wonder this distorted concept doesn't appeal to them!

Perhaps they haven't learned that God offers quality as well as quantity — all they have ever longed for, all they have never attained, the very life of God Himself, made available. Whatever the cause, such ignorance is truly costly, and Christ says to them, "If you only knew the gift of God!"

If unbelievers only knew the Lord Jesus — how close He is to them at this moment, how ready to accept them just as they are, how eager to draw them to Himself! To them He has seemed at best far-off, disinterested — not a Friend who cares, a Savior who can deliver, a Lord who wants to manage their lives. How much they miss by not knowing the Giver!

But we Christians are often tragically ignorant, too. For all our knowledge of spiritual things, most of us seem abysmally unaware of all God offers us; our knowledge of the Giver Himself is greatly limited.

Pardon we know, and cleansing we rejoice in. But the "all things" of Paul's question ("How shall He not with Him also freely give us all things?") is theory, not practice, with us. The fruits of the Spirit do not come to us automatically, as though we were members of some spiritual Fruit-of-the-Month Club, with delivery guaranteed at regular intervals. God's gifts are for those who know what He offers and who covet those gifts, claim them, and cultivate them. Our poverty-stricken experience testifies to the fact that we do not know what God wants us to have! Our knowledge of the Giver is often both limited and distorted. This is surely the costliest kind of ignorance.

Ignorance of the Giver is the really deadly thing. For all our orthodoxy and for all the glibness of our pious vocabulary, Christ is often little more than a name to us — a shadowy figure in the distance, alive but not very real. He's there, but He's not often a vital factor in our decisions or in our setting priorities. We live much of our lives without reference to Him, and we turn to Him only when we are at the end of our rope. If only we knew how very near He is, how desirous of being reckoned on in every experience of our lives! Our ignorance at this point robs us of the fellowship we need and of power we cannot do without. In other words, it's costly!

No one needs to remain ignorant in this sense. The gift and the Giver are close at hand right now, waiting only to be acknowledged and appropriated. If we ask, He will give — not just anything, not just everything, but the thing we need most every minute. Best of all, He'll give us Himself — the greatest Gift.

People or Pigs?

When the choice is stated so plainly as in the title "People or Pigs?" it seems almost too ridiculous to think about. It takes little time and no special wisdom to recognize that one human being is worth an untold number of swine.

In actual life, however, the issue never seems quite so clear-cut and the choice never quite so easy. The value of the human soul is somehow not so evident; pigs — or any other material possession — seem to acquire a beauty and a desirability which make us loath to give them up.

This is what must have happened on that day in the long ago when men were faced with this strange choice (Mark 5:1-20). The news had spread quickly through the town that the man who long had been the scourge of the neighborhood was completely transformed.

Everyone knew his story. He had terrorized the community day and night. All feared this strange creature who lived among the tombs in the local cemetery, and no one had been successful in shackling him. But now, he was changed completely and was sitting, clothed and in his right mind, with his Deliverer.

So far, so good. No one could deny the benefits of the change, to the man himself or to the whole town. But suddenly a new factor entered the picture. In the process of the man's transformation, a great number of swine had been lost. Now a choice had to be made. It was all well and good to have the problem cases of the town suddenly made into respectable citizens — but what about the swine? If by any chance it was impossible to have both, which would they choose? Would it be people or pigs?

They chose the pigs. And to realize the terrible nature of their choice, it isn't necessary to dramatize the undesirable features of these animals, or to point out, as commentators do, that the keeping of pigs was, after all, an illegal business by Old Testament regulations. Had the swine been beautiful creatures, free from all the disagreeable features usually associated with them, and had the keeping of them been perfectly legitimate, the choice which was made would still be terrible. Faced with the alternative of people or pigs, they chose pigs!

But it's too easy to condemn their sense of values. The point is that the same strange choice is made in our day. Christians are convinced they ought to get the Gospel to every creature and that God wants this done quickly. But somehow, when they have to choose between doing their part in the task of world evangelization or grasping after more of this world's goods for their own selfish enjoyment, it is usually the latter alternative that wins out. They know that men everywhere need the Gospel and that Christ expects His people to get that Gospel to those who are lost without it. But the pigs . . .

Of course, they don't look like pigs, or the choice would be different. If a Christian young man — insisting on devising his own plan for his life instead of seeking the Lord's perfect will — could see the real nature of his choice in the light of eternity, he might choose differently. If a Christian businessman — tempted to keep on increasing his earthly possessions while telling himself that he can't afford to do anything more for the missionary cause — could see with the eyes of God the need of the world, and the strangely pig-like appearance of the material possessions he so covets, he might reach a different decision.

If the Christian woman — convinced she can spare no more time to pray for the servants of God and the missionary cause — could know the verdict of eternity on much of her seemingly endless round of activity, she might suddenly realize her sense of values is no better than that of the people who chose swine rather than transformed men. We are all faced constantly with the choice of people or pigs; our difficulty is that, blinded by the false standards of the world around us, we fail to see the choice in these terms.

To be honest, we must go one step further. What those folks of long ago chose was not pigs in place of people, but pigs in place of Christ. If it came down to a choice between earthly possessions and the Lord, their decision was made. And at least this must be said for them: they knew they couldn't have the pigs and Christ. But we seem to think we can somehow serve God and mammon at the same time — even though our Lord assures us it's impossible.

Plainly, a choice must be made. If the good news of Christ is to be made known to every creature, if the purposes of Christ are to be fulfilled, if the church of Christ is to complete the task for which God has us here, then Christian people must acquire a new standard of values. We will have to forswear softness for the sake of doing His will.

We will have to see our choice for what it often is — an ill-fated attempt to prove that our lives do consist of the abundance of things we possess. We will have to learn that these material possessions not only fail to satisfy us but, even worse, also take our eyes off the real reason for our being here. In short, we will have to choose Christ — and people — in place of pigs.

It will often be a hard choice. The issue won't stay settled; the choice will crop up in an infinite variety of forms. To choose Christ and His will instead of pigs will seem a costly business. But we will be glad throughout eternity if we choose wisely — more wisely than those poor souls who preferred pigs to Christ.

An Ex-Priest's Disappointment

An Ex-Priest's Disappointment

He was a babe in Christ. Six months before, as a Roman Catholic priest, he had learned anew the truth of the Gospel and embraced it for himself. Now he determined to prepare himself to help others know his newfound Savior. It was sheer joy to watch him digging into the Book, and it was even greater delight to see him responding to its teaching.

One day he faced an embarrassing predicament. Invited to give his testimony to a group of pastors, he did so with alacrity. A question period followed, and his responses were direct and forthright. Then someone asked, "In your new relationship with us evangelical Christians, have you experienced any disappointments?"

He tried to parry the question. It was obvious he didn't want to answer it. He pleaded his newness in the Christian life and begged to be excused from replying. But his questioner persevered; there was no escape.

Hesitatingly, he admitted two disappointments. As he described them, he spoke with the same intensity with which he had testified a few minutes before to his conversion experience.

How would it be to see the Protestant church through the eyes of one so recently a part of it, after years of service in Roman Catholicism? What faults would he see in us that we had failed to see in ourselves? We listened intently to every word.

For one thing, he said, he missed a sense of reverence in Protestant worship. He didn't have to spell out his disappointment to us or document his charge. Our minds were already busy filling in the details, validating all he said and more beside.

We had heard the distracting buzz of pointless conversation before, during, and after our "worship" services. We had seen everything that preceded the preaching treated as "preliminaries," and how the preaching itself was considered more a test of the minister's ability to capture our attention than a word from God for our needy hearts. The music we had so often tolerated in our services seemed now like an offense to God and to the sensitive ears of many like our friend, the ex-priest. The trite, meaningless lyrics; the self-centeredness of much of our "praise"; the mindless way in which we mouth great truths set to music — all these things we remembered in a moment of time. We were ashamed.

So we had no zeal to argue that our friend was wrong. Nor did we have any words to assuage his disappointment; we could only share in it. And resolve that, God helping us, we'd do something about it.

He shared with us another source of disappointment: the lack of humility that seemed to characterize his evangelical brethren. He explained he wasn't accusing them of pride, in the usual sense of the word. Rather, the thing that concerned him was the attitude of us evangelicals toward divine truth — an implicit impression that we know it all, possess it all, have nothing new to learn from God or man about the things of eternity. He illustrated his point by saying that, if the Roman Catholic Church in the days of Luther and Calvin had had the grace and the humility to learn of God from these men, what a difference there would have been in subsequent church history!

Again we knew he was right — not just about Rome in the days before the Reformation, but about us. We thought of our tendency to equate the infallibility of the Word of God with the infallibility of our interpretation of that Word. We thought of our readiness, as conservatives, to defend secondary and tertiary doctrinal positions with the same zeal and vehemence we brought to a defense of the fundamentals. We remembered observing liberal groups where, despite an erroneous view of the inspiration and authority of Scripture, men seemed more earnest in their study and searching of the Book than we did. *Could it be* that we thought we had learned all there was to know of the things of God? Did we think we had a stranglehold on God's truth? Did we give that impression to others besides the ex-priest?

Years have passed since I first heard this man confess his dual disappointment. But I cannot forget what he said. Lack of reverence, lack of humility — may God forgive us and help us to mend our ways!

Spectator — or Servant?

Once a year the sights and sounds of Christmas dazzle and even overwhelm us. We delight in the beautiful carols and the pageantry of star and shepherds, of manger and magi.

But when the Apostle Paul writes about how "love came down at Christmastime," he doesn't allow us the luxury of being mere spectators as the cosmic drama unfolds. Instead he draws a profound picture of what it meant for Christ to leave heaven at that first Christmas season, then charges us to "let this mind be in you, which was also in Christ Jesus" (Phil. 2:5). It's as though he were saying, "If you are really a Christian, you can't be a spectator; you've got to be a servant."

Now servantship isn't easy. That's why so few of us achieve it. It's also why we settle for being spectators at Christmas, rather than the participants God calls us to be.

What kind of "mind" led Christ to leave his place of glory? What kind of "mind" are we meant to have if we are really to follow him? In the second chapter of Philippians, Paul gives us a glimpse of what all this meant for Christ — and of what it may mean for us.

Paul insists Christ's decision to become a servant was voluntary. All heaven's riches were His, and if He was to become poor, it would be by His choice. Just as He would later say, on the threshold of dark Calvary, "No man taketh [my life] from me. . . . I have power" (John 10:18). Thus from the beginning it was true that servantship was thrust upon Him by no one —

not by man, not by the devil, not even by His Father. He chose it.

And so it is with us; no Christian has to be a servant. We can spend our days rejoicing in our blessings, uttering occasional pious thanksgivings for our salvation, living out our lives in relative comfort and security. In other words, we can enjoy the Christmas drama as spectators. We who have been made rich in Christ are not compelled to become poor servants; there is an easier way, and most of us prefer it to servantship.

Indeed, down through the ages most professing Christians have taken the same route — the easy one. Because this is the way the majority of Christians live, we can drift into it, too, without fearing reproach from our fellow believers. But if "this mind" — the mind of Christ — is to be in us, and if we are to become His servants and the servants of needy men, it will be because we choose to become something besides spectators.

Paul won't let us forget, either, that Christ's choice was costly. "He humbled Himself" — and what mere human being can put enough content into these words? We may only guess at the cost involved. At best, we shall always underestimate the price He paid to become a servant.

Consider, for example, what it must have meant for Him to exchange the beauty of heaven for a world made ugly by its inhabitants, by the defilement and degradation caused by their sins. Who can reckon how much this cost him?

I stood one day in one of the slum villages which constitute the "belt of misery" encircling a large city of South America. Thousands of people lived there, crowded into crude shacks made of cardboard, straw matting, and cast-off tin. There was no beauty — not a blade of grass, not a flower, nothing but unrelieved misery. There was no water, either, except that hauled in tins from a distance. Wherever I looked there was nothing but barrenness and desolation and the pitiful "homes" of thousands of people.

I thought of the comparative comfort my home affords me — a touch of beauty to delight the eye, an adequate shelter from the elements, a host of little things that make life pleasant. I wondered if I would ever be willing to exchange all that for what I was looking on then. I asked myself if I would ever let go what I cherish to take, instead, that which was inherently so repulsive to me. Suddenly I was reminded of the One who left glory I couldn't dream of and came to corruption such as I couldn't imagine, in order that He might be both a Servant and a Savior. In some sense, I had a new concept of the costliness of Christ's decision. And I heard an insistent voice say to me once again, "Let this mind be in you, which was also in Christ Jesus."

It's hard to picture what it meant for Him to leave behind the glorious harmonies of heaven to thrust Himself into the shrill dissonance of earth. To hear the choirs of angels and then to hear in their place the jeers, the crudities, the obscenities, and the blasphemies of men — who can reckon the cost of such a decision?

Yet He faced that cost and paid it. And on a lower plane, some of His followers make the same kind of costly decision. I was greatly blessed and convicted a few years ago by reading Bill Milliken's account of his experiences as a Young Life worker in the slums of New York City. He aptly called his book *Tough Love*. It was the story of a decision to leave the comforts of suburban life for the ghetto, where love is so often rejected, where goodness is so frequently reviled, and where Milliken's reward for providing food and shelter in his apartment for the kids of the streets was the bitterness of having them steal his possessions and mock his love.

106

Once again I had a glimpse of the costliness of the decision Christ made and which He calls us to make, if we're to be servants rather than spectators. It is this mind — the mind not afraid to pay the price of servantship — to which He summons us.

But servantship is not the end of the matter. Paul will not allow us to forget that the Father highly exalted His Servant-Son. That is, Christ's decision was not only voluntary and costly, but also rewarding.

Supremely that reward came to Him when He returned to heaven's glory. But He needn't have waited until then to receive a foretaste of His reward. There was one day, for instance, when He saw a money-grabbing tax collector abandon his lucrative job in order to follow Him whose only treasure was in eternity. And there was a day when a woman, whose moral reputation was bad and whose life was undoubtedly worse, caught a glimpse of forgiving, accepting love and went off a new person, with His kindly admonition to "sin no more" forever ringing in her ears. The Servant was already receiving reward!

It hadn't been easy to become a servant, but surely He was recompensed when one whom He had served stood firm, when so many others had fled away, and declared, "Lord, to whom shall we go? thou hast the words of eternal life" (John 6:68).

And what more could Christ have asked for than to hear His Father speak to the sons of men and say, "This is my beloved Son, in whom I am well pleased" (Matt. 17:5). Reward enough!

The Father still has rewards for those who give up the easy life of spectators to become servants. It isn't easy to put yourself at the disposal of another, especially when your service seems so often to be unappreciated. But "God is not . . . unmindful" (Heb. 6:10 *Weymouth*), and He graciously rewards His servants, not only in the sweet by-and-by but also in the tough here-and-now.

Not always, but sometimes, he who receives a cup of cold water from us looks up in gratitude — and we are amply rewarded. On occasion, we are allowed to see a seed we have sown spring into life and become a fruitful plant. Then we know it has been more than worthwhile being a servant. If someone we serve finds it easier to trust Christ because we have demonstrated His love to them, we are well paid indeed!

There are times when He lets us know that we have pleased Him, whether or not our service has man's appreciation. To bring pleasure to His heart, to fulfill His expectations for us, to be in some small measure like Him — this is all the reward any of us may ask. He does not deny it to those who, like their Savior, choose to be servants rather than spectators.

Great Preacher

I've heard some great preaching in my time. I'll never forget the beauty and power of Dr. J. Gresham Machen's stirring message based on the familiar hymn, "There Is a Green Hill Far Away." With utter simplicity, yet tremendous profundity, the New Testament scholar expounded the hymn, phrase by phrase, in a way that made the Gospel crystal clear; the grace of God shone as a glorious thing.

Forty years have passed since I heard Dr. Samuel M. Zwemer, apostle to the Moslems, extol the saving power of Christ to a college congregation. But the memory of the heart-warming way in which he proclaimed the Good News is fresh with me today.

Nor will I ever forget some of the matchless expositions of Scripture I heard from Dr. Donald Grey Barnhouse. He coupled a deep, personal understanding of God's revealed truth with an amazing ability to illustrate the Scripture in a way that illumined our minds and reached our hearts and wills.

These were great preachers — men whom God gifted in a special way and who spoke to the hearts of multitudes. But my favorite preacher is none of these. Towering above them all, it seems to me, is John the Baptist. A book should be written about John as preacher. Note a few characteristics of this man's preaching that evidence his greatness.

For one thing, he preached for results. When his message was finished, his hearers knew action was called for — there was something they ought to do because of what they had heard. They weren't always sure what their response should be, but they knew something had to be done. As a result, they couldn't be satisfied with just shaking his hand and mumbling, "That was a good sermon you gave us today, Pastor," or "What a challenge!" or even "Better luck next time, Preacher!"

Instead, they knew that John — and the God whose messages he preached — was expecting them to respond to the truth they had heard. There was something in John's presentation which many a twentieth century churchgoer has yet to learn:

— that God's Word demands action;
— that a challenge is really a challenge only when there's a response;
— that God seeks more than an intellectual assent from us.

It's a good preacher, a great preacher, who gets that across to his congrgation.

We see all this in the third chapter of Luke. John preached forthrightly, simply, clearly; and the multitudes, the tax-gatherers, the soldiers all had the same question: "What shall we do?" John's message was demanding, and all three classes of hearers knew they must give some kind of response to what they had heard.

And John had an answer for their question — a different answer for each group. Nor was his reply couched in mealy-mouthed, glib cliches. He didn't tell them to go home and pray about what their response should be. He didn't suggest that, if they'd just consecrate themselves a little more, God would be satisfied and they would be happy. Instead he answered them in the same down-to-earth, practical manner that characterized his whole message.

Look, for example, at his reply to one group: "Well, if you've got two coats, give one to someone who has none." His hearers must have been stunned. They probably weren't expecting that kind of answer. But they had asked what they should do, and John the Baptist told them — in such simple, direct fashion that they couldn't mistake what God was saying to them. They could follow John's counsel or they could reject it — but to their dying day they would have no doubt what he had called them to do.

I preached about John the Baptist one Sunday morning at a Bible conference and mentioned his forthright reply to his hearers' question. That afternoon, strolling about the conference grounds, I met a lady who said, "I just want you to know that your sermon on John the Baptist this morning has spoiled my whole day."

I assured her I really hadn't planned to do that and then asked her how I accomplished it. Her reply was direct: "Well, ever since your sermon this morning, all I can see is my clothes closet back home!"

John the Baptist would insist this is an appropriate response to a message. Sermons are not meant to be enjoyed; they are intended to make demands on us, to affect our thinking and our conduct, to elicit a response at the level of our everyday living. God intends that His Truth change our attitudes and our actions.

So I honor John the Baptist for the fearless way in which he proclaimed the Word of God. I am reminded by him that the proper response to any revelation from God is, "What shall I do?" I learn from him that God looks, not for a nebulous, theoretical response from me, but one that works itself out in my relationships with Him and with my fellow human beings. In getting these basic points across to me and to others, John has shown himself to be a truly great preacher.

God's Delightful Surprises

God delights in surprising us. Again and again He does what we least expect Him to do. His word to us, in many of the strange circumstances of our lives, turns out frequently to be different from what we had anticipated.

Herein lies the built-in excitement of Christian living: we are in the hands of One whose words and deeds are always consistent with Him, but often at variance with what we expect. I was meditating on this fact recently when I discovered an excellent statement of it in a sermon by Dr. Harold Englund, then pastor of the First Presbyterian Church of Berkeley, California.

"Jesus is full of surprises," Dr. Englund wrote. "Just when you think you have Him categorized and understood, He says the unexpected and your system is revealed as obsolete. Just when you think you have the Lion of Judah in a cage, safe, known, a part of your philosophical or religious landscape, you suddenly realize that it is you who are in a cage bound by the bars of your own limited expectations."

Surely the words which Jesus spoke to His disciples just before His ascension came as a great surprise. Their future seemed dreadfully uncertain; it is hardly likely they were prepared for His words to them, as they are recorded in Acts 1:8. Can't you picture the surprise — even the shock — registered on their faces as He spoke of Jerusalem, Judea, Samaria, and the uttermost parts of the earth?

Jerusalem — that focal point of all the hatred against their Lord and against them! Samaria — were

112

they to be witnesses to those religious mongrels? And what would the phrase, "unto the uttermost part of the earth," mean to this little group, to whom a journey of a few score miles was an event long to be remembered?

Yet a few years later these surprised disciples were serving Christ in all these strange places. By God's direct leading and by the force of divinely controlled circumstances, they had scattered to the ends of the earth — His witnesses in places where they had never dreamed of going!

It may be He wants to surprise you, too — if you don't allow yourself to be "bound by the bars of your own limited expectations." If you make yourself fully and unreservedly available to Him, He may well take you to places you've never dreamed of going and use you in ways you haven't imagined.

We honor God when we expect the impossible from Him, when we look to Him to do in us and through us that which defies human explanation. To those who thus trust Him, how delightful are His surprises!

The Problem of Priorities

For most of us, there just is not enough time in the day to do all we want to do. Nor enough money in the bank to meet all the financial demands made on us. And no matter how young we are, or tireless, our energy always seems to run out before we accomplish everything on our agenda.

What's the answer? Is it found in "moonlighting" so we'll have more money, or in pep pills so we'll have more energy, or in rushing about frantically trying to cram more into our waking hours than we ever could before?

We've all tried to solve our problems in one or another of these ways. And we've all proved no ultimate answer is found just by increasing our supply of dollars or by stretching the hours at our disposal or by developing new sources of energy. Somehow these remedies leave us still woefully short of all the things we need to meet the demands of life.

Our real trouble lies not in the shortage of time or money or energy. The problem is priorities. The challenge, specifically, is how to make the best use of the time we have, of the money already at our disposal, of the energy which for the strongest of us is nevertheless limited.

It's a complicated business, this matter of priorities. If it involved only choosing the good and rejecting the bad, it would be easy. But life is seldom that simple. A host of good things clamor for our time, and only a few of them can be crowded into the hours available. Which ones should we choose? Which ones will give the best return on our investment of time?

The same problem faces us with regard to our bank accounts — no matter what size they are. There is an overwhelming number of good causes clamoring for our support, and our funds will stretch only so far. Where will our gifts do the most good? What investments will pay the best dividends, both temporal and spiritual?

Then, since there are limits on our energy, no matter how many vitamins we take, and since we can't do everything, what *shall* we do?

Often the real battle is not between the Good and the Bad, but between the Good and the Best. We haven't time to read all the good books in the world, so we need to know which are the most beneficial. We can't give to every good cause, so we have to discover where our gifts will accomplish most. We may wear ourselves to a frazzle doing good things, so we must decide which things are most worth doing.

Which is another way to say we daily face the problem of priorities. Behind that problem lies the need for discernment — how to know what is important and therefore worth spending ourselves on. One writer has this in mind when he counsels us, "Most people don't need a course in speed-reading so they can read faster; they need to know what not to read!"

Paul knew the Christian would be grappling with priorities every day; when he prayed for the believers at Philippi, he asked God to give them the gift of discernment — the ability to "distinguish things that differ" so they could "approve that which is excellent." The great apostle knew that these dear people would be plagued by the priorities problem. Their only hope of spending their lives and substance was for God to enable them to distinguish between the multiplied claims made upon them.

We need the same kind of discernment today — and only God can give it. We are bombarded with appeals; the communications media are constantly at work, reminding us that there are countless ways to spend our money, to fill our waking hours, to use our limited energies. The sobering thing about all this is that the choices we make will determine not only our happiness in this life but also our rewards in the life to come.

Moreover, our priorities need continual readjustment in the light of Scripture and of eternity. "Wherefore do ye spend money for that which is not bread? and your labour for that which satisfieth not?" was the probing question of the Old Testament prophet (Isa. 55:2). By his query, he was saying, "Wake up! You've got the wrong priorities."

So do we. Yet God will answer the prayer for discernment in these matters if we know how desperately we need it. He will help us see that some things we thought were important are not so significant after all. He will change our sense of values, reminding us that, with limited supplies of time and energy and money, we can't afford to fool around with what is merely good, when we might be involved in that which is best.

Sometimes a person's priorities change in a moment of time. A man is told by his doctor that he probably has only six months to live. Instantly he knows that some things are very important which just a few minutes ago seemed secondary. Some things which previously claimed his attention now seem insignificant, even worthless, in the light of the news given him.

Some years ago I sprained the third finger of my left hand while playing volleyball. The next morning the finger was puffy and sore, and the doctor advised keeping an ice pack on it. By evening it was swollen more than ever and had become discolored. The doctor took one look at it and said, "We're going to have to cut off your wedding ring."

At first I thought it was a joke. When I saw that the doctor was serious about the matter, I protested, pointing out that I had worn that ring for over thirty years and wasn't about to have it cut off.

The doctor, unimpressed by my protest, replied at least half seriously, "If we don't take the ring today, we may have to take off your finger tomorrow!" It didn't take me long to make that decision! I almost shouted, "Take the ring then."

In a moment, my priorities changed. The ring had seemed very important until I discovered I might have to choose between it and my finger. The ring was still a good thing, highly prized, but my finger was more important; to choose between the two was easy.

If we ask God for discernment, as Paul did on behalf of the Philippians, He will give it to us. He'll help us know what really matters. He'll keep us from fooling around with that which is merely good when we may be involved in the best. He will help us deal with the problem of priorities. We'll still have only twenty-four hours in a day, but we'll use those hours in the way His wisdom dictates. He may not increase our income, but He'll enable us to use what we have in the wisest way. And though we may never have enough energy to suit us, we'll have enough to do all the things He wants us to do.

Judgment — for Us?

It isn't a popular idea. You probably haven't heard
a sermon on it recently. Chances are you haven't
really thought much about what it means. But Peter
was outspoken on this theme. Forthrightly he declared, "Judgment must begin at the house of God"
(1 Pet. 4:17).

Judgment on unbelievers — yes! Judgment on
Christ-denying religious teachers — inevitably! Judgment on a world system that has exchanged God's
truth for a lie — this, too, must come. But judgment
at the house of God, judgment on the church of Christ,
judgment on us, the conservatives, the fundamentalists,
the evangelicals — Lord, this be far from us!

There's a reason for our neglect of this text, of
course. It has always been easier to see the mote in
someone else's eye than the beam in our own. Self-
judgment is always costly, so we escape it whenever
we can.

It is easier to condemn the deadness and fruitless-
ness of other churches and churchmen than to face
these blights in our lives. The former attitude is cheap,
the latter costly. But there is no hope for effective
service of our own until we see ourselves under the
judgment of God, until we engage in the bitter business of self-judgment. For this, as Peter says, "the
time is come."

Then, too, it is much easier to blame the world for
not listening to our message than to ask whether we,
rather than the message, are the real stumbling blocks
to unbelievers. There is an offense of the cross inherent in the Gospel that ever remains a stumbling

block to godless men. But there is another cause of stumbling — a self-righteous, loveless proclamation of doctrinally sound propositions — enunciated without the power of the Spirit, without the love of Christ, void of identification with the headaches and heartaches of men. This kind of offense is not inherent in the Gospel. Yet much of the world's apathy, antagonism, and unbelief today is traceable to the fact that the messengers, not the message, have become the great barrier to belief. It's time for judgment — beginning at the house of God.

Moreover, it is always easier to lament the moral standards or ethical fuzziness of unbelievers than to judge by the Word of God our own choice of reading or TV viewing or level of conversation. No revival will come to our lives until we stop judging others long enough to judge ourselves. To admit that Christ is lord over the leisure times of our lives is for most of us theory, not practice. Judgment, beginning at the house of God, is called for.

To mention only one other realm: the sins and shortcomings of the ecumenical movement are obvious to many of us. We judge that movement by the Word of God — and so we should. But this is a much easier undertaking, a much less costly exercise, than facing up to the deplorable divisions, the bitter name-calling, the refusal to pray and plan together that characterizes so much of our conservative, evangelical world. It is readily apparent to us that many of the ecumenists have lost the Scriptural teaching concerning the Body of Christ. But to point out the faults of others does not absolve us of blame!

For all our knowledge of the Word, have we not failed miserably to understand and to demonstrate the unity we so piously claim to possess? The time is past when we dare to excuse our seeming inability to stand together for the Gospel of Christ and to move ahead together for the evangelization of the world in our generation. To claim unity in Christ, as we do so vociferously, is not the same thing as having it and certainly not the same thing as manifesting it. Judgment draws near, not only to an ungodly world and misguided religionists. It draws near, first, to the house of God.

Dare we face that fact — and not tremble? It may be we will not see unbelievers confessing their sins until we confess and forsake our own. God's call to His people is not to judge others — but to humble themselves.

The City, As God Sees It

The City, As God Sees It

In our day, big cities are a headache. Name any one of them, and inevitably there is conjured up a picture of pollution and poverty, decay and danger, violence and death, in both physical and spiritual senses.

A big city is a place to be escaped from. We move out of it as soon as our economic situation permits us to do so. Commuters by the millions spend their days in the concrete jungles, then flee from them when evening comes. City churches watch their congregations dwindle and long for greener fields in which to serve the Lord.

I mention this as observation, not condemnation. In any case, it seems unlikely these trends will be reversed in the near future. But as Christians amid such conditions, we're called upon to remember at least two things: (1) when we flee the city we don't escape our responsibility for it; (2) the city looks very different to God from the way it looks to us.

It may be that the truth of Isaiah 55:8, 9 ("My thoughts are not your thoughts, . . . saith the Lord. . . .") is nowhere more clearly demonstrated than in God's attitude toward the city as contrasted with our viewpoint. The Book of Jonah gives us an amazing portrait of the Lord's urban attitude — a portrait that well serves to challenge our wrong ideas and correct some of our superficial thinking.

The city in question is, of course, Nineveh. This was actually a complex of cities, in this respect not unlike modern New York City, one authority suggests. Nineveh was noted for its size, public works, and paganism. But the big question is, how did God look at this concentration of men, buildings, and wickedness?

You don't have to look far in the Book of Jonah for your answer. On three different occasions God calls it a "great city" (1:2; 3:2; 4:11); in another place He calls it "an exceeding great city" (3:3). These are not the claims of the local chamber of commerce; it is the God of the universe who calls Nineveh great — despite the fact He isn't impressed by our human standards of greatness. We have a right, therefore, to ask a further question: what causes God to call this city great?

The Lord is not unduly impressed with the size of this city or with its awesome buildings. It did cover a tremendous area — some authorities believe it was twenty miles long by twelve miles wide. Its buildings were almost overwhelming to the human eye; its walls, according to some historians, were the height of a ten-story building and crowned with some fifteen hundred towers, each twenty stories high.

This is greatness by man's standards, but not by God's. Centuries later Christ warned of the utter impermanence of man's monuments and buildings (Mark 13:2). His words in this regard might well be written over the towering structures of Metropolis in our own day.

Not size, not buildings, but people: this is what impressed the Lord, according to the last verse of the Book of Jonah. God, who values a single soul more than all the riches of the world, is impressed by the great numbers of people who swarm about the city; He obviously expects Jonah — and us — to be similarly impressed.

Those thousands of people are His handiwork — His children by creation, if not in the full, biblical sense of sonship through redemption. God deals with them as individuals, but He also sees them in the group — a great concentration of people upon whom He wants to pour out His love. He is fully aware of all their waywardness and human limitations. But He has made them; through all the ruin brought upon them by the Fall and by their own disobedience to Him, He still sees greatness.

Surely He sees the cities as the gathering places of multitudes for whom Christ gave His life. As J. B. Phillips has reminded us, ours is the visited planet — the place to which the Son of God came in the flesh, forever thereby revealing His love for each creature and for the great multitudes of them who huddle together in the shadows of Metropolis. It is these people — as they are and as they can be through the grace of God — who confer greatness upon any city.

Moreover, God sees Nineveh not only as it is but as it could be. It could be a wonderful place where happy people live in fellowship with the God who made and redeemed them. He sees the potential of their lives, once they are reconciled to Him and devoted to doing His will. This to Him is greatness, and so He calls Nineveh — and all its modern counterparts like Tokyo, London, Rome, New York — "great."

But God sees the city as not only great, but also needy. Specifically He sees Nineveh, and our present-day versions thereof, as needy in three ways.

First, the city needs a message concerning the Judgment of God. It is to this ministry He called Jonah (1:2 and 3:4). How delinquent we are in delivering the message of judgment to the cities of our day! We are content to list symptoms without denouncing their causes. We bewail the sickness of our culture, but we seldom announce the judgment of God upon it. We like to blame the disturbed condition of cities and nations on Communism or secularism or another convenient scapegoat. All the while God has been calling us to proclaim His judgment against the conditions which make Communism so attractive to the downtrodden masses of needful people.

He wants us to pinpoint the reason for the sense of alienation which haunts men and fills them with frustration and futility. But, like Jonah, we cringe from this task and flee to our own Tarshish, hoping to avoid the awesome demands of a message of judgment.

Moreover, it's not enough to blame the conditions in our cities on sin in some general sense, either. That's too cheap, too easy. We ought to ask, "What kind of sin has brought this chaos?" and "Whose sin is this?"

Shouldn't the Christian be concerned, for example, about air pollution as well as drug traffic? Doesn't God hate both? And if He does, shouldn't His judgment be pronounced equally against the man who exploits the environment for commercial gain and the one who, for similar motives, exploits the addict?

If we truly represent His righteous judgments, our zeal for law and order will be directed against both power-hungry corporations and the mindless violence of radical youth groups. The city today, as in Jonah's day, needs to hear of the judgment of God; that word must be heard in the skyscrapers and luxury hotels and in the hovels of the ghettos.

If we are gripped by a sense of God's judgment against sin, we will be concerned deeply about the self-ishness of those who, possessing much of this world's goods themselves, make it impossible for the poor to escape their economic and social bondage.

If we could see the city as God sees it, we would see a place desperately in need of judgment at every level of its life.

But God saw that Nineveh needed something else: it suffered not only for want of a message, but also for want of a messenger. The city will not hear the message of God's judgment in some miraculous or automatic fashion. It needs a missionary, a man of God who knows he is sent to the city to proclaim God's judgment there.

This seems like an inadequate solution for Nineveh's problem, doesn't it? And who would dare to tackle the illness of our great modern cities in this way? One man to cope with a tremendous city, steeped in its own corruption! One man against the incalculable forces of godlessness — an unequal match, if ever there was one!

Yet this is where God wants to start, in Nineveh and in your city. One person in your neighborhood — plus God.

That's exactly how the problem of the city is being tackled in many places today. I've met men who have heard that kind of call from God; they are marching in the name of Christ, but seemingly alone, against the entrenched wickedness of great cities. They march in Philadelphia, in Newark, in Boston, and in a host of other places.

Outwardly it looks like an exercise in futility. Actually God is demonstrating that He's not looking for multitudes to serve Him. He's proving what His mighty power can accomplish with a handful of available people.

That's what God wants! He prizes our availability more than our ability. But, like Jonah, we too often have other plans. Tarshish looks so much more attractive than Nineveh. Having decided that, we find ways to rationalize our disobedience while God continues to weep over cities which need messengers of His judgment and grace.

The Lord knows the city needs a message and a messenger to bear it. He sees, too, that above all else it needs redemption. In the heart of God, judgment is reserved only for those who will not have His deliverance. He has no pleasure, Ezekiel assures us, in the death of the wicked. He wants to see Nineveh drawn to Himself, transformed by His power; He will go to any lengths to bring this to pass.

That, of course, is what He wants for your city. He wants you and others like you to be changed. Then He wants the changed ones to be agents of change. He's ready to show His power in common, ordinary stuff like Jonah and you and me; He's ready, too, to transmit that power through us to others. Nineveh doesn't have to be the way it is — nor does your city!

We all agree God can transform men and even whole cities. Nothing is beyond His power, we piously declare. But in the same breath we tell ourselves that such a thing is impossible today. Jonah may have had a theoretical confidence in the power of God to change men and cities, but in the face of Nineveh his confidence crumbled.

Likewise, we become experts in explaining why there is no hope for the cities in our time. We cite the awesome, overwhelming power of entrenched evil; we point to the tragic weakness of the people of God and the pathetic smallness of our forces. As a result, there is little hope for our present-day Ninevehs — not because the city is so big or its evil so great, but because the expectation of God's people is so small, and their faith so limited.

God never forgets the individual, but He does not think solely of him. He calls Jonah because He has Nineveh in mind. He pursues one man because He can't forget a needy city. And He wants that city, not merely for its own sake, but for what it can do for a needy world.

So God has been good to you, but in dealing with you He has not been thinking only of your good. When He saved you, He had others in mind as well — individuals and towns and even cities He wants to reach. You are part of His plan for reaching them.

If only we may see this! What a change it would make in our lives to realize that He saved us in order to save others! And what this concept would do to dispel the purposelessness and consequent frustration and boredom which seems to characterize so many Christians today!

Does all this say anything to us? Can we see ourselves in Jonah, called of God to the great city but hurrying off in the opposite direction? It may well be God included the story of this disobedient missionary in His Word in order to give us a new sense of responsibility for those places of unloveliness from which the church has fled.

The mission fields of the world are not all located in foreign lands and across great expanses of salt water. The cities for which God yearns are mission fields as truly as any other place to which we ordinarily apply that term. Some of us who will never go to distant shores may well be called, like Jonah, to go to the cities, to weep over them as our Lord did, and to claim out of them a people for His name.

We need to see the cities, not as they show themselves in headlines and newscasts, but as God sees them. Seeing them in this way, we will find our place in God's plan for reaching them with the good news of an abundant life they have never known — which they will never know apart from Christ.

There is hope for Nineveh. It is a hope solidly based on the compassion and mercy of a God who never changes in His love toward His creatures who eke out lonely lives in the cities.

Like Nineveh, your city needs a message of judgment. It needs a messenger unafraid to face overwhelming odds in the name of Christ. It needs new creatures helping others to become, through Christ, new creatures. The city needs you.

The Tragedy of Hopelessness

When hope is gone, nothing remains. The third chapter of Acts tells the story of a helpless cripple by the Temple gate — a man whose case is doubly pathetic because he has evidently resigned himself to his tragic situation. With a dull and listless gaze, he beseeches the passersby for alms.

No doubt there had been a time when things were different — when he still possessed a lingering hope that somewhere, somehow, he might walk again. Now he would settle for something, anything, that would help him keep body and soul together and thus sustain him in his misery. He expected nothing more than that, and he gained nothing more. The last thing he was looking for, on this memorable day, was healing. He surely didn't anticipate that this was the day when salvation would come. In his own eyes, his condition was hopeless.

In this sense he was like people all around us today. They may once have hoped for joy, peace, a sense of purpose in this life, and some assurance concerning the life beyond. But no more. Escape is now the watchword. They settle for anything that will ease the pain of existence, silence the accusations of conscience, help them forget their yearnings for better things. Even temporary relief is a boon, and they seek it anywhere. This is the fruit of hopelessness.

As Christians we should not be surprised or shocked if men without hope seek temporary relief in foolish ways. You might do the same thing if your outlook were as hopeless as theirs. I once heard a Christian general say, "I'm not surprised when my officers head for the bar at the end of a grueling day. They don't know where else to turn for help."

When a man is told he has an incurable disease, when his body is racked by unendurable pain, he will take the narcotics prescribed even though he wouldn't think of touching them if he saw hope in any other direction.

So men in our own time will settle for a palliative — anything, however temporary, however deadly in its ultimate effects, if only it seems to offer momentary relief. The pleasure-mad society of our day seeks surcease from any direction, perfectly willing to endure the inevitable "morning after" for the sake of a brief interlude of forgetfulness. Call these people short-sighted, if you will, but don't be surprised at their behavior; don't forget that you would act the same way if you had no spiritual resources. This is the normal way to behave when all hope is gone.

And don't be surprised if, in their hopelessness, they seem not to be crying out for salvation. They have a spiritual hunger, but they know not what it is or what causes it. "Salvation" is a foreign-language word to them. These persons have long since ceased to hope for any help from heaven; they are so abandoned to hopelessness that they beg for coins rather than for Christ.

But remember — no man is hopeless in God's eyes. If this man at the Gate Beautiful had been as hopeless a case as he thought he was, Peter and John would never have paused on their way into the Temple. The beautiful story of Acts 3 would have gone untold. The cripple had given up, but God hadn't given him up. In heaven there was still hope.

Given the fact that God doesn't write off sinful man as hopeless, the tragedy is that so many of His followers do. Too often we drop people from our prayer lists, convinced there is no hope for them. Too quickly we give up witnessing to our hardened, pleasure-bent loved ones and neighbors, believing there is just no possibility of their ever knowing the Lord. We write off whole areas of the world as impossible, allowing ourselves to be overwhelmed by the seeming hopelessness of the situation. We accept men's verdicts concerning themselves rather than God's verdict, and we thus sin against God and our fellowmen.

God hasn't given them up. Is there someone you've been calling "hopeless"? Do you dare to continue to call Christ "Lord" and at the same time allow yourself to disagree with His verdict on the situation? Are we right, or is He? The world is full of men who think of themselves as being without hope and full of other men who think their fellowmen are hopeless. But that same world is ruled by a Savior who will not accept men's verdicts concerning themselves.

If He will not, we dare not.

What Does "Go Ye" Really Mean?

Usually we think of the Great Commission in purely geographical terms. Result: a missionary is someone who has been transplanted from one environment to another.

The Great Commission does have geographical implications. Because the church has interpreted it this way down through the years, Christ's servants have risen up, left home and country behind, and gone to strange, far-off places for His sake and the Gospel's.

But is this all that "go ye" means? Does one have to cross salt water or learn a strange language to be obedient to the Lord's command? Not necessarily! There are men and women who have never been called to a strange land, have never been led out of their professions or occupations. Yet they are missionaries, conscientiously fulfilling the purpose and program of Christ. Christ has summoned them to go — not to a new country, but to their fellow workers and friends, there to bear witness to the glory of His Gospel.

These are laymen — God's redeemed children, called to salvation and service. Theirs is not what is usually called "full-time service," but "full-time" it is and "service" it is, because Christ has called them and they have gone with His Gospel — to the factory, to the schoolroom, to the hospital. We have learned in many of the so-called mission fields of the world that only through mobilizing the laity for effective witness can the world ever be evangelized. In like manner here in the homeland, Christ will be truly made known to needy men only when we learn that "go ye" means something more than geography.

Here's a surgeon, known for his professional skill. The operating-room nurses have noted something different about him. They are accustomed to the sudden hush that comes over the operating room just before he begins his work. His head is bowed; he is at prayer. It is not ostentatious, but there is a clear confession of the doctor's dependence on his Savior. To nurses, patients, fellow doctors, he is a man who loves Christ and is unashamed of his Lord. He has heard Christ's "go ye" and he has gone — to the operating room. Thus the Gospel is proclaimed in a place where it might not be heard otherwise, because of his obedience.

An office worker quietly lives a holy life before his colleagues. He speaks a word for Christ whenever the Spirit gives him an opportunity, but he knows this witness is valuable only as his life confirms it. He asks the Lord to use his life and his lips for the glory of God. He is not completely surprised, therefore, when one day a fellow worker says to him, "There's something different about you. I've watched you for a long time, and I want what you've got." Thus the Gospel is proclaimed to a man who might otherwise never be reached, because his office colleague recognizes that "go ye into all the world" means the office and the factory, not only Africa and Argentina.

A group of retarded children are patiently, tenderly taught by an earnest young Christian. In their own way, the children know that she cares for them and loves them, and they respond to this love. Something more than compassion motivates this woman; she is there because she has heard Christ say, "Go ye," and she has gone.

The room at the end of the hall in the university dormitory is a popular gathering spot. A grad student lives there and serves as dorm counselor for that floor. The other students find it a good place to visit; they get a hearing for their problems, sympathetic understanding, and often a word that points them to the only true source of help. The grad student is there, not just to earn extra money toward his tuition, but because for him Christ's "go ye" meant a dormitory mission field.

These are not hypothetical cases. They are real people — laymen I have known. They are men and women who heard the Great Commission and responded. These are missionaries — whether the local church or anyone else recognizes them as such. They are part of a wonderful thing God is doing throughout the world today. He is saying "Go ye!" and men and women who have never been to a seminary, who will never know the ordination of men, are responding to the commission of God and are going with the Gospel to hospital, to homes, to factory, to college.

Are you one of them?

A Crucified World

A crucified Christ we know, or we would not be Christians. We have learned something from the Word, at least theoretically, of the crucified self; we have often read — and believed — Paul's words, "I have been crucified with Christ."

But do we know anything of a crucified world? The apostle also said that by the cross of Christ the world was crucified to him (Gal. 6:14). We have quoted the phrase often; it is almost too familiar to us. But is there any sense in which, in our daily lives, it is apparent that the world has been crucified to us?

Paul's use of "world" here obviously has no direct reference to geography or to population. He is thinking of the world as a godless system, the manner of life of men and women who live in the flesh, with no vital relationship to Christ. This manner of life, with all its ambitions and aspirations, its idols and appetites, its desires and pleasures — this he sees now in its true nature, as he has seen this world in the light of the cross of Christ. At its best it now appears to him a loathsome thing, a convicted criminal, put to death on the cross. "The world," he testifies, "has been crucified unto me."

Has anything like that happened to us? We have learned to hate the grosser manifestations of sin. Perhaps we are not deceived, as so many are, by the tinseled trappings with which man tries to make the best of his earthly existence. By the fact of our knowing Christ, some of the world's charms have lost their attraction. Yet there are few of us indeed who can honestly say the world has been crucified to us.

Look how much of our time is spent on the transitory, the passing scene. Note how frequently our affections are set on things of the earth — not on the loathsome things, to be sure, but upon *things*, as though our souls could ever be satisfied with that which the world vainly feeds upon. To this extent, the world is not crucified to us.

Do we still secretly covet the praise of men, still care (more than we would like to admit) about being well-thought-of by men? Do we live as though the "Well done!" of men was more to be prized than the same words from the lips of the Savior? If we want anything more than we want His approval, the world is still with us, uncrucified.

Much of the time even we Christians live as though this life were everything, our own little concerns supremely important. When the things of time blot out those of eternity, when our thinking so often centers on what we need, what we want, what pleases or displeases us — when that happens we are thereby confessing we know little of the thing Paul talks about.

It is altogether possible to be completely separated from "worldliness" (as the church has too narrowly defined it) and still be chained by the world's more subtle attractions. These things are legitimate, we tell ourselves, and then become so involved with them we never seem to have enough time for fellowship with the Lord. This, too, is worldliness, even though it may be one of its more attractive — thus more deceptive — forms.

This business of seeing the world in its true light is not a luxury of the Christian life. If we fail to recognize the world for what it is, we testify we do not truly apprehend the meaning of Christ's cross. He died to set us free from the world's blandishments (Gal. 1:4). His death was intended to deliver us from living unto ourselves — even our best selves (2 Cor. 5:15). A great day dawns in our spiritual experience when we behold the world in the light of the cross, when all its subtle deceptions, all its foolish pretensions are revealed to us, and we learn to hate all that belongs to it.

This is the key to the problem of getting more people to serve the Lord at home and abroad. Let a man see the world for what it truly is, and it's not hard for him to give himself for the Lord's service. The task of world evangelization awaits the rising up of those who, abiding in the shadow of Christ's cross, have learned to look out on the world through His eyes.

Nor would there be any problem in financing the Lord's work if the world were crucified to us. No shortage of funds exists for the task, except as they are diverted to the lesser things of time and sense. And what a volume of intercessory prayer would go up on behalf of the Lord's servants, if time now spent by Christians in serving the world was released for investment in the things of eternity!

For the Apostle Paul, the preciousness of Christ made all else seem like refuse. For him the things of earth had grown strangely dim. Have they for us?

Inexcusable

Our standard method for dealing with difficult situations is to seek the easiest possible way out. So when the disciples were confronted with a hungry mob that seemed too big to feed, they threw up their hands in despair and saw no solution except to send the people away, to let them fend for themselves. They pleaded with the Lord Jesus to get rid of the problem by dismissing the crowd.

But this was no real solution, and the Savior knew it. His challenging reply to His disciples was, "They need not depart; give ye them to eat" (Matt. 14:16).

He was saying, of course, that there was no excuse for the people remaining hungry. He knew His power was adequate for the situation if His disciples would only trust Him. The problem was not something to be evaded but to be faced and dealt with, in the light of His will to feed the crowd and His ability to do so.

Spiritual famine is inexcusable, too. Over every missionary map — over every table of awesome statistics telling of the great multitudes in the world who still perish of spiritual hunger — should be written the words of our Lord Jesus: "They need not depart."

We have all sorts of explanations why a great part of the earth still starves for the bread of life; we endeavor to salve our consciences by repetition of these excuses. But the Lord will have none of our rationalization. He knows there is no reason for spiritual famine except the unbelief and disobedience of His followers.

God has provided both the Gospel and every

necessary means for its propagation to the ends of the earth. The starving throngs perish, not because of the will of God, but because we have tried to get rid of the problem by ignoring it or passing it on to someone else. Christ's word is still "They need not depart."

And His word is still "Give ye them to eat." He puts the responsibility back on His own, not because their power will ultimately feed the throng, but because His power will do it in response to their faith and obedience. We may always think of numerous reasons why we cannot fulfill His command, but those "reasons" are really excuses if we truly have an all-powerful Lord.

We talk of closed doors, of limited opportunities; He says, "Give ye them to eat." We bemoan our shortages of funds and personnel. He still asks only the opportunity to demonstrate what He can do with what seems an utterly inadequate supply.

It is not enough to confess the sins of past generations or to lament their slowness in carrying out the Great Commission. For the sins of the church in other ages we do not have to answer. For the fact that multitudes remain unfed we will have to give account before God.

The world can be evangelized in our generation. There need be no shortage of funds for the task; our Heavenly Father "holdeth the wealth of the world in His hands," and He also has entrusted so much of that wealth to His children in our day. There need be no shortage of personnel; never were so many fine Christian institutions of learning producing so many young people prepared for His service.

Besides, the Lord of the harvest still answers the prayer of faith for the thrusting forth of laborers into the harvest. There need be no shortage of instruments, of equipment for the work. God seems to have showered upon our generation a special abundance of tools, some of which no other generation possessed, to accomplish the task.

Best of all, God's power has not waned. No one who has seen God provide miraculously for His work in our day has difficulty believing the story of the five loaves and two fishes. He is still in the business of transforming our inadequate resources into a great sufficiency for the fulfillment of His purposes. With such a God, the multitudes of our day need not go hungry. We can feed them, and we will be without excuse if we fail to do so.

It's Not Too Late!

It often looks too late. The tides of godlessness are strong in our day. Evil in its most concentrated forms surrounds us. Darkness, intense spiritual blackness, envelopes the world. In the midst of it all, the church seems woefully weak, dismally apathetic. An unbelieving world plunges headlong for hell while Christians seem unable to utter more than a whisper of warning or to sound even the faintest note of hope.

But it's not too late! Things looked at least this bad in the dark days just preceding our Lord's death on Calvary. There simply didn't seem to be time or strength to stem the tide of iniquity.

Christ came to His own, and already they had rejected Him. They mocked His matchless love; they surrounded Him with hatred on every hand. As He made His way into Jerusalem, there were a thousand reasons for believing nothing further could be done — but Christ refused to accept them. Read again the amazing story as it is recorded in Luke 19:41-48. It says something important to our day, something we need to remember right now. It says, "It's not too late!"

It's not too late to weep. Our Lord Jesus not only wept with those who wept (like Mary and Martha, in John 11); He also wept with those who didn't weep but should have. Jerusalem was too far gone in its spiritual blindness to weep for itself. Yet a lonely figure looked upon the city (Luke 19:41), and the love of His heart overflowed in tears.

In our day, many Christians bemoan the condition of the world. But this is not the same as Christ's

142

weeping over Jerusalem. It's easy to condemn others, and all too easy to resign ourselves to apathy; anyone may do these things. But only a heart filled with compassion can look lovingly upon our times and see how close to the kingdom — and how far from it — the nations are, and weep. It's not too late for that.

Nor is it too late to do something about the church. It need not be the pathetically weak instrument it is. But what is called for is neither a pious condemnation of its weaknesses nor a passive coming to terms with them. Something more drastic is needed at this late hour.

So it was that Christ cleansed the Temple in the last week of His earthly life (Luke 19:45, 46). He had done it before at the beginning of His ministry; but these issues don't stay settled, and here He used the fleeting minutes shortly before His death to do it again.

He recognized that there was no use weeping over the city if nothing was done about the Temple. Was He not reminding us that, in our own day, "the time is come that judgment must begin at the house of God"? (1 Pet. 4:17). There is little point in weeping over the city if we are not ready to deal ruthlessly with our own failure, as individuals and as the church.

It's not too late to deal firmly with our petty jealousies, our grasping ambition, our carping criticism of brethren, our coldness and our apathy in the face of a desperate world. These attitudes and actions were once driven from our hearts, but unobserved they have crept back again. The real problem in our day, as in Christ's, is not the city — but the temple.

Finally, it's not too late to teach. Our Lord taught day after day during that fateful last week (Luke 19:47). Somehow He felt this wasn't wasted time; to teach the people was a worthy use of these precious hours.

143

Today the same kind of ministry is called for. In our churches, let the teaching ministry be paramount. In our homes, let neighborhood Bible classes be formed. In our family circles, let us find time to learn together from the Word of God. In our contacts with men, saved and unsaved, let us seek opportunities to teach the Word of God. The hour is late — too late for many things — but not too late for this.

Out of the long ago there comes a call to the church of Christ — to weep, to cleanse, to teach. For these things, it's not too late.